In the Long Run

In the Long Run

A Study of Faculty in Three Writing-Across-the-Curriculum Programs

Barbara E. Walvoord
University of Notre Dame

Linda Lawrence Hunt
Whitworth College

H. Fil Dowling Jr.
Towson State University

Joan D. McMahon
Towson State University

With contributions by

Virginia Slachman
University of Cincinnati

Lisa Udel
University of Cincinnati

National Council of Teachers of English
1111 W. Kenyon Road, Urbana, Illinois 61801-1096

Manuscript Editors: Robert A. Heister, David A. Hamburg
Humanities & Sciences Associates

Production Editors: Peter Feely, Michelle Sanden Johlas

Interior and Cover Designs: Doug Burnett

NCTE Stock Number: 56428-3050

It is the policy of NCTE in its journals and other publications to provide a forum for the open discussion of ideas concerning the content and the teaching of English and the language arts. Publicity accorded to any particular point of view does not imply endorsement by the Executive Committee, the Board of Directors, or the membership at large, except in announcements of policy, where such endorsement is clearly specified.

Library of Congress Cataloging-in-Publication Data

In the long run : a study of faculty in three writing-across-the-curriculum
    programs / Barbara E. Walvoord . . . [et al.].
        p. cm.
    Includes bibliographical references and index.
    ISBN 0-8141-5642-8
    1. English language—Rhetoric—Study and teaching—Evaluation.
    2. Interdisciplinary approach in education—Evaluation. 3. Academic
writing—Study and teaching—Evaluation. 4. English teachers—Rating of.
I. Walvoord, Barbara E., 1941–   .
    PE1404.I4 1996
    808'.042'07—dc20   96-28320
                                                                  CIP

This book is dedicated to

Our faculty colleagues, whose story this is, and whose generosity allowed us to tell it.

The administrators on all our campuses who have supported and funded the writing-across-the-curriculum effort, especially, Hoke L. Smith, president of Towson State University, and Patricia Plante and Robert Caret, provosts; Joseph Steger, president of the University of Cincinnati, Norman Baker and David Hartleb, provosts, and Anthony Perzigian, acting provost; Arthur De Jong and William Robinson, Whitworth College presidents, Darrell Guder, dean of Academic Affairs, Kenneth Shipps, provost, with special appreciation to Tammy Reid, associate dean, co-writer of the original CAPHE grant, and an effective, longtime supporter of WAC.

The staff members and student assistants in WAC offices whose daily labor undergirds all we do in WAC.

And finally, our personal friends and our families, who have supported and encouraged us in the long, long run that was this project.

Contents

List of Illustrations

1 Introduction and Review of Research

"This workshop was excellent."

"This has been the most energizing and inspiring two days I have spent. . . ."

"I was a little disappointed that nothing was said about 'criteria' or 'keeping up standards' or whatever in formal writing, or in peer review, or in drafts."

"I came to this workshop with some reluctance. . . . However, I was happily surprised."

"I learned; I enjoyed; I ate well."

"I felt like [the workshop leader] didn't really understand the intensity of the problems some of us face in student journals."

"I am going to use informal writing in my classes."

"I'm all fired up about trying this, and I can see many applications for it."

"The ideas are restricted by large class size."

"There was a lot of variation, which allows for a lot of flexibility in implementing this."

"I plan to start tomorrow."

Perched on the edges of their chairs, faculty are writing these comments in the last few minutes of a two-day writing-across-the-curriculum (WAC) workshop. Minds buzzing with stimulation, rear ends sore from sitting, belts bulging from donuts, spirits warmed by collegial communion, they write down their plans and their hopes—and sometimes their skepticism—about writing across the curriculum.

WAC began twenty-seven years ago, apparently at Central College in Pella, Iowa, where Walvoord gathered an interdisciplinary group of faculty to discuss student writing (Russell 1991; Steele 1985). Since then, thousands of faculty in institutions of higher education nationwide have similarly participated in WAC workshops, discussion groups, "fellows" programs, team-teaching programs, writing-intensive courses, linked courses, and other permutations, many of which are described in Fulwiler and Young's *Programs That Work* (1990) or

McLeod and Soven's *Writing Across the Curriculum* (1992). Perhaps a third or more of U.S. institutions of higher education have writing-across-the-curriculum programs (McLeod and Shirley 1988; Stout and Magnotto 1991). Among those institutions are the three very different ones profiled in this study—small, private Whitworth College in Spokane; comprehensive Towson State University in Maryland; and the University of Cincinnati, a large, public research institution that also includes several two-year and open-admissions colleges.

What has happened in the long run to WAC faculty within these programs? What did faculty expect from WAC when they entered into it? After two, five, or fifteen years, what have the workshops and other WAC activities meant to them? How has WAC affected their teaching philosophies, attitudes, and strategies? How has it affected their career patterns?

The authors of this book came together to try to address those questions. We are longtime directors of WAC programs or graduate assistants in those programs. Our associations go back a long way—back to 1981, when Walvoord moved to Baltimore and joined Dowling in the first five-week Summer Institute of the newly formed Maryland Writing Project; back to their shared leadership in the Baltimore Area Consortium for Writing Across the Curriculum (Walvoord and Dowling 1990); back to 1984, when McMahon joined Dowling in the Towson State University WAC program; back to 1989, when Hunt invited Walvoord to lead WAC workshops at Whitworth College in Spokane; and back to 1991, when Walvoord began directing the University of Cincinnati's WAC program, to be joined there in successive years by graduate assistants Slachman and Udel.

In 1993, Hunt proposed to Walvoord that they collaborate in collecting WAC faculty stories, building upon the collection that Hunt had already published at Whitworth. Walvoord brought in her research at the University of Cincinnati, where she and several graduate assistants had been using questionnaires, interviews, small-group discussions, syllabi, and other teaching documents to investigate WAC's impact on faculty. She also brought in research from Towson State, where Dowling had done classroom observations and written about the history of the WAC program and where McMahon had taken a sabbatical year to interview Towson WAC faculty and publish a book of their teaching strategies.

Thus, not only had we co-authors been longtime associates within the WAC community, but we each had been studying WAC outcomes and gathering WAC faculty accounts on our own campuses for a number of years. From 1993, when we decided to write this book, we gathered further interviews and faculty-authored accounts from all three institutions.

Previous Studies of WAC's Impact on Faculty

We were, of course, not the only ones who were asking, "What happens to WAC participants in the long run?"

"Match-to-Sample" Studies

One group of WAC outcome studies is what we call "match-to-sample." That is, researchers ask whether faculty, after WAC workshops, adhere to WAC beliefs or use WAC strategies, such as journals, that the *researchers* have defined as central to WAC. In other words, do faculty match the WAC-defined model or sample? The usual data are faculty questionnaires or interviews, sometimes augmented by syllabi and assignment sheets, classroom observations, or questionnaires to students about classroom practices.

An example of these match-to-sample studies is Smithson and Sorrentino's 1987 investigation of thirteen of the eighteen faculty who had attended a workshop at Virginia Polytechnic Institute and State University. On a Likert scale, faculty indicated their agreement with WAC principles and classroom practices which the authors had formulated (e.g., "Writing cannot be used to teach concepts in the subject disciplines but only to test if concepts have been learned" [338]). This survey was administered before the workshop, immediately following the workshop, after ten weeks, and after five years. At the ten-week and five-year points, ten of the faculty also responded in writing to queries such as "Did you continue to use writing to teach your subject?" and "If you use fewer methods now than you did during your first quarter after the workshop, which ones have you dropped and how soon after the workshop did you stop using them?" These more open-ended questions still emphasize "using" or "dropping" the methods which the workshops or researchers had defined. Even five years after the workshop, the faculty reported using more of the writing strategies than they had before the workshop. Reports from 238 students in ten classes affirmed their teachers' use of methods which the researchers had defined. For example, 86 percent of the students stated that their teachers provided for peer evaluation of drafts. Students provide another source of data, but the emphasis is still on whether faculty are using researcher-defined WAC strategies.

Other studies which fall at least partially into the match-to-sample model are Goetz (1990), Kalmbach and Gorman (1986), and Hughes-Weiner and Jensen-Chekalla (1991). In this last study, holistic scoring of 1,200 student essays also revealed a small, but statistically significant, positive correlation between the number of WAC courses a student had taken and his or her essay score. Braine's 1990 study of faculty teaching writing-intensive (W-I) courses without having had WAC workshops showed that most were not using WAC strategies.

Taken as a group, these match-to-sample studies suggest that after workshops, many faculty use what WAC researchers define as WAC classroom strategies.

These findings are useful, but they exhibit several significant problems. The first is the role of the researcher. Some of the studies were conducted by the same people who directed the WAC program, yet the researchers are usually cast as neutral collectors of data. Often, they do not describe their own roles or political contexts for the study.

A second problem with the match-to-sample studies is that, within the foundationalist paradigm of this research, where researchers are supposedly finding out whether faculty *really* used the WAC strategies, faculty self-reports through surveys and even through interviews are considered weak. Eblen (1983) notes that "self-reports may blend respondents' beliefs and intentions with actual practice" (347). Actual practice is the assumed goal. However, it is possible that the beliefs and intentions are what we really need to know. For such questions, self-reports *would be* strong data.

Further, match-to-sample studies imply a perhaps overly simplistic "training" model: the workshop "trains" faculty to do something that the leaders and researchers know or assume to be good. To "prove" that WAC strategies enhance learning is problematic at best (Ackerman 1993), though a body of education research does firmly establish that interactive strategies such as having students write, responding frequently to student work, getting students involved in learning, and having students work collaboratively do enhance learning (Chickering and Gamson 1987).

A related concern is the assumption that even if WAC *is* good, the more of it faculty do and the longer they continue to do it after the workshop, the more successful the workshop is judged to have been—a rather primitive measure of effectiveness.

Match-to-sample research raises troubling issues of power. For example, who controls the creation of knowledge—the researcher or the teacher? Whose voice is privileged in the report? How are "data" produced, defined, and used? What political and social agendas, what cultural contexts, and what factors like class and gender are influencing the research? WAC workshops themselves often have striven for collegial relations in which power and "expert" roles are shared. The philosophy of the National (Bay Area) Writing Project (NWP), which has impacted many WAC programs, deliberately eschews leaders who dictate good practice and train teachers to do it. Instead, their philosophy holds that workshops tap teacher wisdom, everyone learns, and changes in practice emerge from reflection and dialogue.

The dissonance between such an egalitarian philosophy and match-to-sample research arises in an interesting way in Bratcher and Stroble's (1994) study of workshop impact on K–12 teachers. The *findings* of this study are minimally relevant to us because K–12 teachers operate within much different contexts than college faculty. But its *methodology* raises important questions. The researchers summarize the NWP's egalitarian philosophy. To them, it presents a research problem because the NWP offers no set definition of good practice. So the researchers construct one—a sophisticated version of match-to-sample, in which faculty are rated not just on whether they are *using* a particular researcher-defined strategy, but on the *degree* to which they are using it. The degrees are labeled "ideal," "acceptable," or "unacceptable" (74). The researchers have thus defined not only specific strategies but a level of use as their goal. Ironically, then, the research on NWP workshop outcomes has imposed a judgmental frame that the NWP workshop philosophy itself eschews.

A related problem with the match-to-sample model is the role of change. Match-to-sample research assumes that the workshop achieved the desired change and then the faculty member stopped changing. The more WAC strategies the faculty member is using and the longer he or she uses them, the better. There is no room in this paradigm for the faculty member to make new contributions by developing attitudes or practices not listed by the researchers' questionnaire. There is no room for the role of change suggested by the growing literature on "faculty vitality." Vitality is often defined and measured by faculty output of research, teaching, or service or by other evidence of faculty engagement, motivation, and involvement. Martin Finkelstein says, "Vital faculty are faculty who are not only motivated, but also are able to identify opportunities or potential opportunities and take advantage of them" (1993, 2). The literature on faculty vitality suggests that the most vital faculty are continually changing across their careers and that one of their changes is to "experiment with alternative teaching strategies" (Baldwin 1993, 14). We need to ask: How might vital faculty use a WAC workshop? As a "training" experience? As a *developmental* experience? Would their subsequent changes continue to match a model that WAC researchers might construct?

Another body of research raises similar questions about the role of change for WAC faculty. Rogers (1983) and others have traced how "innovations" get "adopted." They characterize "early adopters" as people who are willing to take risks and try new things, and who are horizontally networked—that is, within the university setting, who are networked with colleagues inside and outside their disciplines. If faculty who attend WAC workshops can be classified as "early adopters," and if they come to WAC partly because they like new ideas and are not averse to taking risks, might we not assume that after WAC they might risk trying other good ideas that come to them through their broad networks? Or do we in WAC think that we have a corner on all the good ideas about teaching they would ever want to try? Do we think, as Bratcher and Stroble do, that we can identify four criteria which we consider "central" to good WAC pedagogy and then judge faculty compliance as "ideal" or "unacceptable"? Is it appropriate to have, as Bratcher and Stroble do, the stated goal of teachers' "full implementation" of *our* model (1994, 86)? If these faculty, years later, have continued to change so that they no longer conform to our model in the ways our match-to-sample tests are able to show, does this mean the workshops have failed?

These match-to-sample studies, then, raise several problems: the role of the researcher and the political uses of the research; the foundationalist assumptions that neutral researchers are finding the real truth; the role of self-reports; the training model; the assumption that researchers know what good teaching strategies are; the dynamics of power between researchers and teachers; and the issue of faculty change—its meaning, its value, and its role in WAC outcomes.

Open-Ended Questions about Change

A few WAC studies have asked faculty open-ended questions about change and about WAC's role in spurring change. Such questions allow the researcher to move away from some limitations of the "match-to-sample" model. Open-ended questions also *leave to the faculty* the judgments about cause and effect that are so important to WAC leaders and so hard to establish empirically. One study that asked faculty to identify change is that of Eble and McKeachie (1985). During the late 1970s and the 1980s, the Bush Foundation supported faculty development, including a number of WAC programs, at twenty-four institutions of higher education in Minnesota and the Dakotas. Through the use of questionnaires, Eble and McKeachie asked a random sample of faculty at these institutions the following question: "Did [the faculty development program] have an effect on teaching?" Of the 455 faculty solicited, 383 responded (an 84 percent return). Seventy-eight percent of the respondents replied, "Yes." Similar results emerged from Kalmbach and Gorman's (1986) study at Michigan Technological University and from Beaver and Deal's (1990) comparison between faculty at an institution that had an active WAC program and one that did not.

Together with the match-to-sample research, these broad questions about change suggest that faculty not only use WAC strategies, but believe that WAC has led to change and improvement in teaching and learning. However, a problem with such broad questions about change and improvement is that they lack informative detail about the complexity of classrooms and faculty lives.

Case Studies

A body of case-study research offers such detail. Sipple's (1987) study, using think-aloud tapes, of how eleven workshopped and eight unworkshopped faculty planned an assignment suggested that planning by workshopped faculty included a larger, more clearly defined repertoire of strategies for planning writing assignments. Workshopped faculty used assignments to aid student learning, not just to test knowledge, and they integrated writing with learning.

A number of case studies focus on classrooms rather than on the course-planning process. They provide rich detail about the complexities teachers face when they try to use WAC strategies in the classroom. We will argue, though, that these studies often retain the problems of voice, power, and defining good, which were typical in match-to-sample studies. We will propose that a new sort of study is now needed.

One case study of WAC impact on faculty is part of a study of WAC at Radford University. Kipling and Murphy (1992) usefully portray the institutional context and the career history of several Radford University faculty. The authors' accounts of several faculty members' development over time show their struggles, resistance, questioning, adaptation, and change. The accounts, based on faculty logs, essays, interviews, and close working relationships with the authors, are replete with faculty voices. Within that context, the point of the chapter on faculty is to show how several initially reluctant faculty became converts (our term). All the faculty are described as finally "having come to see," as the chapter's last sentence puts it, what WAC was trying to demonstrate. The influence of the "conversion story" or "testimonial" genre is evident. It is worked out through the authors' selection of which faculty to portray, through the words of the faculty themselves, and through the way the authors arrange, select, and frame the faculty stories.

The testimonial genre is also strong in various collections of faculty stories and faculty accounts of successful classroom practices, which are not always couched as research but nevertheless add to our store of knowledge about outcomes (e.g., Fulwiler and Young 1990; Parker and Goodkin 1987; Griffin 1982; Thaiss 1983; and numerous articles that can be located in ERIC by using the descriptors "writing-instruction," the name of the discipline, and "higher-education"). Sometimes these accounts present actual classroom assignment sheets, syllabi, student work, or student evaluations. Sometimes they report struggle, disappointment, change, adaptation, or abandonment of WAC strategies. Sometimes they (perhaps unwittingly) reveal mixed theories and paradigms for teaching and learning or dissonance between belief and practice. Nonetheless, they often remain largely within the conversion or testimonial frame and paint a rosy picture of how faculty have adopted WAC strategies and how well these strategies work in the classroom. Their aim is persuasion or assistance to other faculty in adopting WAC. The ones published for a wider audience are the tip of the iceberg; its underwater base is the wealth of such stories published in campus newsletters and presented at local and regional conferences.

We are not saying that these accounts are false or that genre influence is wrong. The influence of one genre or another will always be present when people tell stories. But it is important to be aware of the impact of genre influence.

Challenging the rosy findings of the testimonials has been a spate of case studies that investigate how faculty "resist" WAC beliefs and practices and/or how faculty fail to implement them so as to result in student learning. These studies have been valuable in showing the realities of the classroom context and, in some cases, representing the teacher's own voice. However, despite their seeming candor about classroom realities, we will argue that many of these case studies still privilege the voice of the outside researcher, silence the teacher, and reflect the "match-to-sample" paradigm in which the researcher knows best and in which change is desired only in the direction the researcher defines.

One such study is by Swilky (1992), who follows two teachers during the semester after a WAC workshop. She details the suggestions she gave them and notes the ways in which they "resisted" or "adopted" what she calls "my ideas." Her practice of referring to the teachers by their first names casts their quoted words into the frame of a research subject, not a professional whose words are being cited by a scholarly colleague. She points out the dissonance between what the teacher has stated as a goal and what she, the researcher, perceives as actually happening—for example, "By maintaining this approach to responding to student texts, Robert works against his goal of assisting students . . ." (58).

However, *Robert's* views on this perceived dissonance are absent. Did he *intend* to work against his own goal? What was his reasoning? The researcher uses quotations from Robert's letters to her to illustrate "both positive and negative resistance." But the judgments about positive and negative are the researcher's. Although Swilky concludes that "different determinants, including personality, assumptions, beliefs, and institutional conditions, affect teachers' decisions about pedagogical priorities," she does not explore these determinants from the teachers' points of view, but from her own. She does not question the value or rightness of the ideas she gives to the teachers. The article is strangely split in this way, with a nod to the teachers' concerns, but with a dominant paradigm of researcher-controlled WAC orthodoxy, against which teachers are counted as "resisters." "My ideas" still form the sample that faculty are expected to match. The researcher's emphasis is on teaching methods adopted or not, rather than on the teacher's own goals and theories, the teacher's ongoing growth and change, career patterns, or ways of interpreting the data.

Similar is Swanson-Owens's (1986) case study of two high school teachers with whom she worked for a semester on a project to use writing. She constructs a model to explain the teachers' "resistances" to her "suggestions." The model posits that teachers resist because their "locus of attention" and "conditions of instruction" may be quite different from that of the WAC leader. In such circumstances, their resistance is called "natural" but still regrettable. The teachers' adaptations to the conditions and contexts of their real situations are judged as resistance to an assumed ideal, rather than as possibly the wisest or most creative course they could take under the circumstances. The researcher's frame of reference forms the sample which the faculty members resist matching. The model explains why teachers resist, rather than how they develop.

In this group of "resistance" case studies, then, the teacher is still subtly viewed as what Norton calls the "mere implementer, deliverer" of researcher-determined, orthodox WAC teaching strategies (1994, 135). The studies focus more on why teachers resist than on why they do what they do.

Marshall (1984) investigates two high school classrooms—one in science, one in social studies—where the teachers deliberately tried to use writing for learning. The social studies teacher, Marshall concludes, largely accomplished his goals. In the science class, however, students' ways of handling the assignment subverted the teacher's goals, in Marshall's judgment. However, the *teachers'* voices, *their* judgments about their success—or about Marshall's judgment—do not enter in.

Johnstone (1994) details a college geology class where the teacher, though a strong advocate of WAC among his colleagues, does not achieve his learning goals because, the researcher judges, he does not integrate journals effectively into his class but keeps them peripheral, relying largely on lecture and multiple-choice testing. The responsibility for the classroom failure is placed squarely on the teacher. But his voice is oddly absent. We do not learn from his perspective his rationale for doing what he did, nor even whether he concurred with the researcher's judgment.

Several other case studies likewise make the point that teachers' intentions may be subverted in the classroom by students' ways of working, but they study multiple classrooms, and they draw conclusions not about what the individual teachers they studied might have done, but about what teachers in general might do to avoid the difficulties the researchers define—e.g., Marsella, Hilgers, and McLaren (1992); Nelson (1990); and Herrington (1981).

The body of case-study research, then, varies in the level of "resistance" it ascribes to the teachers and the severity of the judgments made by the researchers. What that body of research has not done, however, is to focus on why the teachers did what they did. It does not present the teachers richly to us as people who are struggling, in often complex and skillful ways, to realize their own goals and to juggle multiple constraints within the classroom.

A Model for Our Study

One model for that kind of study is provided by Carneson (1994), who studies elementary and secondary school teachers in Britain. In his diagram of the model he proposes, teachers are shown working among many diverse and even conflicting forces. At the base of the diagram is the teacher's accountability to self, professional colleagues, school management, students, parents, friends, family, and community. The teacher then moves through a "framing matrix" composed of many different perspectives and theories of teaching, not just those of a particular project like WAC. Finally, in the classroom, with all its constraints and stimuli, teachers try to maximize control over elements that are in turn controlling them. In contrast to Swilky's and Swanson-Owens's focus on "resistance" to WAC, Carneson's model focuses on why the teacher does what she or he does. It recognizes that teachers often have very sensible reasons for decisions and are motivated by multiple, powerful loyalties. There's a recognition that teachers are deeply rooted in their own pasts, that they have philosophies, outlooks, investments that shape their use of new ideas. The researcher attempts to illuminate the reasons, goals, and principles that guide teachers' actions and development.

Hargreaves (1988), who also works in K–12 settings, notes the preponderance of "transmission" teaching that relies on lecture and keeps students passive. Most current theories about why transmission teaching is so widespread are "psychologistic," says Hargreaves—that is, they blame teachers' personal qualities or lack of competence; proposed remedies are better selection of teachers and better teacher training. But Hargreaves counters with what he calls a "sociological" explanation for the dominance of "transmission" teaching:

> The framework I want to propose rests upon a regard for the importance of the active, interpreting self in social interaction; for the way it perceives, makes sense of and works upon the actions of others and the situation in which it finds itself; the way it pursues goals and tries to maximize its own (often competing) interests; the way it pursues these things by combining or competing with other selves; the way it adjusts to circumstances while still trying to fulfil or retrieve its own purposes—and so forth. In this view, teachers, like other people, are not just bundles of skill, competence and technique; they are creators of meaning, interpreters of the world and all it asks of them. They are people striving for purpose and meaning in circumstances that are usually much less than ideal and which call for constant adjustment, adaptation, and redefinition. Once

we adopt this view of teachers or of any other human being, our starting question is no longer why does he/she *fail* to do X, but why does he/she do Y. What purpose does doing Y fulfill for them? Our interest, then, is in how teachers manage to cope with, adapt to and reconstruct their circumstances; it is in what they achieve, not what they fail to achieve. (216)

Hargreaves's theory of teacher change is made more explicit later in his article:

All teaching takes place in a context of opportunity and con- straint. Teaching strategies involve attempts at realizing educa- tional goals by taking advantage of appropriate opportunities and coping with, adjusting to, or redefining the constraints. (219)

To Hargreaves's concept that teachers seek to realize education- al goals, Raymond, Butt, and Townsend add the teacher's goal of cre- ating a self:

The process of teacher development has to be understood in relation to personal sources, influences, issues and contexts. While changes in status and institutional mandates provide both possibilities for, and limitations to, . . . development, there is also a deeper, more personal struggle to carve a . . . *self.* . . . Professional development is, in this sense, an enactment of a long process of creating *self,* of making and living out the con- sequences of a biography. (1992, 149)

The WAC studies we have reviewed work from a much more limited and researcher-defined notion of teacher change and develop- ment. They tend to assume that the only change teachers should make is steady change toward WAC-defined ideals. Such a theory is formal- ly proposed in Bratcher and Stroble's (1994) study of sixty-nine ele- mentary and high school teachers, mentioned earlier. Bratcher and Stroble explain their teachers' failure to fully adopt WAC strategies through a developmental model of teacher change. They claim that the teachers they studied through questionnaires, interviews, and class- room observations showed "selective and gradual" implementation of WAC strategies. During the three years that followed their workshops, the teachers moved unevenly, but a general direction emerged. The teachers began with attention to prewriting, planning, and publication opportunities for their students. Then they moved to a fuller focus on rhetorical stance and on student choice and input. Not until later (and at lower percentages) did the teachers attend to revision. The researchers link the teachers' uneven development to their "anxieties and uncertainties" which "blocked their complete implementation of the new paradigm" (83). The "full classroom implementation" of WAC strategies defined by the researchers remains the ideal (86). The researchers fear that teachers "will selectively adopt writing process instructional strategies in ways that fail to honor the paradigm on which these strategies are based" (73). They believe their study shows that full implementation may take longer than expected. We might term this the Pilgrim's Progress model of faculty change, where the researcher measures progress toward a researcher-defined good practice, and the theory of change tries to account for the lack of full implementation. What Swilky and Swanson-Owens called "resistance," Bratcher and Stroble recast as part of a slow and uneven progression toward the goal of "complete implementation."

To summarize so far, there have been three major bodies of WAC outcomes research. One involves match-to-sample surveys based largely on faculty self-reports, augmented at times by other data. That body of research suggests that at least some faculty use WAC strategies after workshops. But that research raises serious questions about the role of the researcher, the value of faculty self-report, the "training" model, who defines what is "good" practice, power in the teacher-researcher relationship, and the meaning and value of faculty change.

In a second type of study, the change issue is addressed by a few studies that query faculty directly through open-ended questions about change and improvement. Most studies suggest that faculty believe workshops have contributed to change and improvement in teaching and learning.

A third major body of research is case studies. They are valuable in showing the complexity of classroom situations. Some are cast in the "testimonial" frame, showing how faculty moved through resistance to adoption. Some show faculty resisting WAC strategies, a useful corrective to undue optimism. But though they provide valuable detail about the complexities of classrooms, these resistance studies, we argue, still assume the match-to-sample paradigm—the researcher defines what is good practice, and the focus of the study is to discover why that good practice was not implemented. Resistance is explained by situational factors that make resistance "natural" or even "positive" or by a regrettably slow and uneven pattern of development toward the ideal. But the ideal remains "complete implementation" of the WAC-defined agenda. Teachers' voices are silenced or contained within narrow, researcher-framed molds. The focus, in Hargreaves's words, is on why faculty do not do X, not on why they do Y.

All three groups of studies, we believe, ignore teachers' "wisdom of practice" (Hutchings 1993, 64); their "practitioner knowledge" (North 1987); the power of their personal vision for their students and themselves (Nyquist 1993); and their right to determine the path of their own career-long development. Further, as McCarthy and Fishman say, "We believe that educational research has too long focused on teachers' supposedly reproducible behaviors while excluding their voices" (1991, 422).

Current education research is moving strongly in this direction, with K–12 studies here and in Great Britain taking the lead (see, e.g., Constable et al. 1994; Hargreaves and Fullan 1992). We believe that WAC outcomes research needs to be informed by these forces.

McCarthy and Fishman's collaborative work, published during a span of several years, provides an example, we believe, of the kind of case study the field needs. In several articles, McCarthy, a writing specialist, and Fishman, a philosopher significantly influenced by WAC, examine Fishman's teaching as it grows and changes over several years (Abbott et al. 1992; Fishman 1985, 1989, 1993; Fishman and McCarthy 1992, 1995; McCarthy 1991; McCarthy and Fishman 1991; 1996). What emerges is the story of a teacher's journey whose outcome the writing specialist does not pretend to know or control, but for which she, and their interaction, provide a rich resource. (Models for such collaboration are described by McCarthy and Walvoord [1988] and by Cole and Knowles [1993].) McCarthy, the researcher, watches keenly and collects data as this fascinating development unfolds. Each collaborator learns from the other. Readers of their accounts learn the complexity of the human journey and share Fishman's reasoning about his classes. Readers also come to understand how Fishman balances conflicting needs, adapts ideas he reads or hears, seizes opportunities, juggles constraints, shapes goals and changes them, combines paradigms and philosophies, but always insists upon his own right to determine what is "good" for him and his classroom.

In one of their articles, Fishman and McCarthy (1992) challenge the fear, expressed by Bratcher and Stroble, that partial implementation of WAC strategies will break the strategies loose from the paradigms that underlie them. Bratcher and Stroble seem to want the classroom to operate unpolluted, within only one paradigm. McCarthy and Fishman argue that Fishman's classroom is a place where different paradigms powerfully interact, shift, change, and develop. Throughout this body of work, Fishman's story leaps from the page in his own powerful words and in McCarthy's observations. His story defies the boundaries of easy generalization; it does not match a sample.

Another case study where teachers' voices enter as co-authors, and their *growth* rather than their resistance or conversion becomes the focus, is a study of four college classrooms by Walvoord and McCarthy (1991) and their college-level teacher collaborators from four disciplines. The teachers, all former WAC workshop participants, collaborated with the outside researchers to study the "difficulties" that arose in classrooms where WAC workshop ideas were being implemented in various ways. The point of the study is not "resistance" in the teachers, but the mutual efforts of teacher and outside researcher to learn what is happening in the classroom and to make pedagogical changes of the teacher's own choosing. The writers suggest that WAC methods discussed in a workshop may work more or less effectively in actual classrooms and that classroom research is one way for the teacher to gain fuller insight upon which to base further pedagogical changes. In the biology classroom, Anderson, the teacher, and Walvoord, the researcher, trace over four years Anderson's pedagogical changes and the subsequent rise in the quality of students' scientific experiments and reports. (Another, differently authored study of Anderson's classroom, focusing on how she manages issues of gender, presents another "take," reminding us of the many viewpoints from which the same classroom may be viewed [see Maher and Tetreault 1994].)

The work of Walvoord, McCarthy, Fishman, Anderson, and their colleagues moves along a spectrum toward investigation not of the "success" of particular WAC-defined agendas, but generally of how teachers change over time, of what factors influence those changes, and of how particular events such as a WAC workshop fit into personal journeys, into broader institutional contexts, and into career-long growth patterns—of why teachers do Y, not why they fail to do X.

Our Approach

We wanted our study to continue this progression. We wanted to get back to some of the large populations of the earlier match-to-sample studies so that we could move beyond individual case studies to see general trends in WAC workshop participants over time. But we wanted to transcend the imposition of a WAC orthodoxy presumed to be good and the adoption of researcher-defined teaching strategies or beliefs as the measure of success. We did not want to interpret teacher change as "resistance" or as regrettably slow and incomplete progress toward "complete implementation" of our agenda. Rather, we wanted to understand WAC's role in teacher-directed, multifaceted, career-long development, driven by the teacher's struggle to define a self, to balance constraints, to maintain control, and to realize educational objectives in ways consonant with that teacher's own personal vision and wisdom of practice.

We did not begin with this desire fully articulated. But, through years of various investigations of WAC outcomes on our campuses, we have moved more and more deliberately toward this vision. We have attempted to listen to faculty in new ways. We invite our readers to listen with us. For that reason, we have tried to pack the present volume with teachers' voices, teachers' stories. We think the present volume will help answer our research questions—what did faculty expect from WAC, what did WAC experiences mean to faculty, and how has WAC affected their teaching and their careers? We think this book will give teacher readers useful classroom ideas, as our faculty tell specifically what has worked for them. The stories tell in teachers' own words the patterns of their lives and thoughts as they struggle to grow across the span of their careers, to realize their own potential and that of their students, and to reflect on what WAC has meant to them in the long run.

2 Context and Methods for the Study

This chapter treats in summary our three institutional contexts, our research paradigms, and our methods. The next chapter contains a detailed section about each institution—its characteristics, its WAC program, and the research methods we used to collect data about its faculty. Readers not interested in the full details can read only this summary chapter.

That next, more fully detailed chapter is arranged institution-by-institution because our methods and data are so intimately tied to the type of institution and to the history of its WAC program; thus they can best be evaluated in that context. Also, we want to show that we have gathered into "*a* study" not only the 1993–1995 data we collected collaboratively since we decided to write this book, but also the bodies of data we collected earlier, during periods of years at the individual institutions, which were never intended to be united—the Humpty Dumpty that never was. Even our 1993–1995 data were influenced to some extent by the nature of each school and its WAC program.

At the same time, we want to emphasize that when we examined our data, the same themes occurred among faculty at all three schools. So the differences among schools largely disappear when we later discuss what WAC meant to faculty and how it affected them.

The Institutions and Their WAC Programs

Our three institutions represent a wide variety, both in general characteristics and in their WAC programs (see Table 2.1). The University of Cincinnati (UC) is a large, research-oriented, state comprehensive university that includes several two-year and open-admissions colleges. It has 36,000 students. Towson State University (TSU) is a Baltimore-area baccalaureate- and master's-level university with 15,000 students. Whitworth College in Spokane is a small, private, religiously affiliated liberal arts college of 2,000. Papa Bear, Mama Bear, Baby Bear. Also midwestern, mid-Atlantic, and northwestern. Public and private. But we don't claim that these schools represent all of American higher education. We have not, for example, included any

Table 2.1. Summary of the institutions and their WAC programs

	University of Cincinnati	Towson State University	Whitworth College
Location	Cincinnati	Baltimore	Spokane
Type	Doctoral, research-oriented, but includes some open-admissions and two-year colleges.	Baccalaureate and master's levels. Large variety of programs.	Baccalaureate with some master's level. Liberal arts.
Students	36,000	15,000	2,000
WAC Program Activities	2-day off-campus *workshops*, 1989–present. 1989–1991, led by Fulwiler and Steffens; after 1991, led by Walvoord. Many on-campus *meetings* and *workshops*. Many *spin-off projects*, e.g., a program that works to create a teaching culture in the departments.	Wide variety of *workshops*, on and off campus, offered by Towson and other area institutions, 1984–present, led by many presenters. Ongoing *small faculty groups* respond to one another's writing. WAC director (Dowling) worked intensively *one-on-one, visiting classes*, etc.	1–5-day *workshops*, 1989–1995, led by Walvoord. Periodic short follow-up *workshops and meetings*. *Team teaching* groups in the CORE meet frequently. Faculty across disciplines *tutor in Writing Center*.
Writing-Intensive Course Requirement	None at present, but general education reform in process will require all general education courses to have a writing/oral/visual communication component.	W-I requirement since 1976.	W-I requirement since 1987, plus team-taught CORE courses with writing component.

historically black institutions, any Deep South or southwestern institutions, and any institution with more than a 15 percent minority population. So this is a study of WAC outcomes within three institutions that are different but not representative of the full range.

The individual WAC programs, likewise, are quite different, though they do not encompass the full range of options. They include programs of varying ages: Towson's began in 1976, Whitworth's in 1987, and Cincinnati's in 1989. Workshops have been used in various ways, and their structure and focus have differed, as will be explained later in this chapter. Each campus has additional unique activities. Directors at each campus have played different roles.

Despite their differences, the three programs have included some characteristics common to WAC nationwide (see Griffin 1985; McLeod 1989):

- workshops and other small faculty groups as the basic entering and sustaining activity for faculty;
- activities such as small-group meetings, team teaching, response groups, etc., intended to sustain faculty over the long run;
- voluntary, not forced, participation in WAC for faculty;
- a writing-intensive, or similar, course requirement (e.g., students are required to take a certain number of "writing intensive" courses approved by a faculty committee);
- collaboration of writing faculty with discipline-area faculty; and
- leadership by a director.

But our three programs do not represent the full range. For example, we have no program where students take a composition course that is linked or paired with a course in another discipline (Graham 1992). Nor do we have "fellow" programs, where disciplinary faculty are assigned a student helper (Haring-Smith 1992).

Our evidence indicates that all three WAC programs have been widely viewed as successful on their own campuses. For example, at all three institutions, media records and conversations with presidents and other school officials indicate that these leaders have regularly cited WAC as one of the institution's stellar programs. Faculty we interviewed—no matter what use they had made of WAC ideas or what criticisms they expressed about specific aspects—almost universally expressed respect and appreciation for the programs. At all schools, over time, volunteer faculty enrollment in WAC activities has been strong. This is a study, then, of the impact on faculty of strong and well-regarded WAC programs that had been in existence from six to eighteen years by the time we finished our data collection.

Our Research Paradigm

We are WAC directors and workshop leaders at our own and each other's schools—change agents who cannot, and do not wish to, stand completely apart from what we study. In our research, we have assumed that there would be no absolute "truth" about the impact of WAC, but that many observers and participants might legitimately construct different interpretations. All interpretations, as well as the data they were based on, would be mediated by language, culture, context, and ideology. However, in constructing our interpretations, we have striven to use research procedures that are accepted as "trust-worthy" in the communities to whom we wish to speak (Lincoln and Guba 1985). We will explain those procedures in this chapter.

In shaping our stance, we have been aided by Argyris's concept of "action science" (1985; 1993), Gitlin's concept of "educative research" (1990), and by the various "criticalist" schools (Kincheloe and McLaren 1994). All of these approaches share three themes. First, research is guided by goals of transforming as well as interpreting the contexts under study. Thus we recognize and accept that an interview by the WAC director with a WAC participant may be data for our research questions, but also may itself shape what we're investigating—the impact of WAC on the faculty member. We believe there is no such thing as a neutral way of observing a natural setting. We chose ways of observing that we thought would contribute to our change goals and research goals.

Second, all of the approaches emphasize that researchers and participants work together to create knowledge and change. Thus we acknowledge that the findings of this study are the product of various kinds of interaction and collaboration between us and the many faculty, students, and administrators who participated in the interviews, classes, and other events from which our data are drawn. It is this interaction and collaboration, we believe, that make our data rich and that help us to understand the WAC participants' points of view.

Third, all three approaches emphasize the importance of revealing the ideological and political foundations of the research and of the situations being studied. We try to do that in the following account.

The Early Data Collection on All Three Campuses

This study's chronology can be divided into two periods—before 1993, when the four of us decided to collaborate on this book, and from 1993 to 1995, after that decision was made. The chronological process of data collection is diagrammed in Table 2.2.

Before the 1993 decision to collaborate, each of us, at our own schools, had been collecting over the years various kinds of data about the outcomes of WAC. (Our data are summarized in Table 2.3 and are discussed in detail in the next chapter.)

The data gathered before our 1993 decision to collaborate included questionnaires and interviews from faculty and students, syllabi, assignments, student work, W-I course proposals, classroom observations by the researchers, faculty-authored articles or conference presentations about WAC experiences, and researchers' participant observations of WAC faculty in small groups or committees where the impact of WAC upon them was evident.

Those data have several characteristics: first, the data had nearly always been used in combination—for example, small-group interviews *with* syllabi and course handouts; faculty presentations *with* syllabi and samples of student work.

Second, the individual campus data included, on each campus, a substantial, open-ended listening component that made us hear the complexity of faculty experiences, faculty voices. We did not rely merely on what, in our introduction, we call "match-to-sample" questionnaires. One of our questionnaires, as we explain in the next chapter, was built from faculty responses to open-ended questions, not solely from researcher-defined options.

Third, in many cases the same faculty members had been followed over time with different types of data, allowing us to "triangulate"—that is, to use one type of data, data source, or research method to augment, check, or question another (LeCompte and Goetz 1982; Lincoln and Guba 1985).

Also unique were the span of years and the number of faculty. The data stretched back over five, six, and, in Towson State's case, eighteen years. We had data of some type on approximately 720 faculty members.

Our Approach to Faculty

Our data allow fascinating glimpses into WAC's impact on departments, institutions, curricula, students, and academic structures, but this study focuses on where our data are strongest: how WAC

Table 2.2. Data collection process

	Separate Data Collection		Decision to Collaborate on This Book	Collaborative Data Collection
	1976 1986 1989		1993	1995
TSU	Interviews, classroom observations, case studies, etc.			
Whitworth		Faculty accounts, team teaching, student response sheets, WAC booklet, etc.		Data collection continues, culminating in 42 interviews and faculty-authored accounts on all three campuses.
UC			Questionnaires, interviews, participant observations, classroom research, etc.	

Table 2.3. Summary of all data

	University of Cincinnati	Towson State University	Whitworth College
Population Studied	Two Populations: *Pop. A:* 117 faculty attendees of two-day workshops led by Fulwiler and Steffens, 1989–1991. (117 = 89% of all those who had attended during those years and were still on campus in 1991.) *Pop. B:* 337 UC faculty who attended two-day workshops led by Walvoord, 1991–1995.	Population: Approximately 200 faculty who participated in WAC activities at Towson or other programs (e.g., Maryland Writing Project). Of these, almost 100 are teaching W-I courses at any one time, though about 50 have never taught a W-I course.	Population: 66 faculty who attended workshops, most led by Walvoord, 1989–1991.
		Types of Data	
(1) Faculty questionnaires used alone, without accompanying interview, documents, etc.	1989–1995: Participant responses completed immediately after 24 two-day workshops. 1993–1994: Questionnaire (Appendix A) on teaching changes mailed to a random 20% of all UC full- and most stable part-time faculty (147 responses = 54% return).	1984–1989: 98 participant responses completed immediately after 6 workshops.	1995: 38 questionnaires (Appendix B) returned by faculty teaching a combined total of 55 W-I classes.
(2) Faculty questionnaires combined with interviews and document analysis.	1991–1992: 101 from Pop. A (Appendix C).		
(3) Syllabi and W-I course proposals.	1991–1994: 18 from Pop. A and 43 from Pop. B: syllabi and W-I course proposals submitted to a faculty committee for approval as W-I courses.	48 W-I course proposals on file.	

Table 2.3 continued

(4) Classroom observation by researcher, combined with interview, consultation with faculty, student interviews, and documents.	1993–1994: 2 classrooms (see Walvoord and Bryan 1995).	1982–1994: 21 classrooms, by Dowling. 1983–1986: 1 classroom (see Anderson and Walvoord 1991).	
(5) Interviews or questionnaires to students in classes taught by WAC faculty.			1989–1991: 1,157 questionnaires (Appendix D) from students in WAC classes during four semesters. 1991: Random group of 16 students in WAC courses, interviewed by Writing Center student consultants.
(6) Faculty-authored articles or presentations about WAC experiences, usually accompanied by syllabi, student work, etc.	1990: 19 faculty accounts in in-house booklet. 1991–1994: 24 articles or conference presentations by Pop. A. 1995: Documentary video, *Making Large Classes Interactive,* produced at UC on how 5 UC Pop. A faculty make large classes interactive.	1991: 18 faculty accounts in in-house booklet. 1985–1994: 11 articles and 48 conference papers and workshops.	1992: 11 faculty accounts in in-house booklet. 1990–1994: 6 presentations by faculty.
(7) Participant observation of small groups of WAC faculty.	1992–94: 43 Pop. A and 23 Pop. B in 90-min. small-group discussions of WAC practices, observed by Walvoord. 4 Pop. A + 7 Pop. B in classroom research groups, led by Walvoord. 33 Pop. A on committees that directly revealed how faculty had been affected by WAC, observed by Walvoord.	1985–1994: approximately 40 faculty in ongoing writing groups, observed by Dowling and/or McMahon. Additional 31 faculty, observed by Dowling or McMahon, in other settings (e.g., W-I course-approval committee).	1990–1994: 7 follow-up workshops/meetings, most with 12–15 attendees, observed by Hunt. Participant observation by Hunt of 9 faculty team teaching CORE courses.

Table 2.3 continued

	University of Cincinnati	Towson State University	Whitworth College
(8) Pre–1994 faculty interviews combined with document analysis.		1991: 18 WAC faculty, interviewed by McMahon.	1990–1991: 12 WAC faculty, interviewed by Hunt.
(9) Final round of faculty interviews and faculty-authored reports, gathered specifically for this book, in 1993–1995. Most accompanied by syllabi and assignments (interview questions, Appendix E).	22 faculty, interviewed by Walvoord, Slachman, Udel, and other graduate students.	10 faculty, interviewed by Dowling and McMahon. (5 of these faculty authored their own accounts.)	10 faculty, interviewed by Hunt.

impacted individual faculty. The individual faculty member, then, is the unit of analysis.

In 1993, when we decided to collaborate on this book, we articulated the approach to faculty that each of us, in different ways, had been reaching on our separate campuses. We did not want merely to measure whether or not faculty were using teaching methods that WAC directors defined. We did not want to separate WAC outcomes from the broader faculty growth and development. Our rich and complex data forced us to see faculty not as adopters or resisters, but as seekers who used WAC as a resource in very different ways, according to their own needs and directions, which we were reluctant to judge. Nearly all the faculty had some points of resistance, often for sensible reasons, and nearly all had profited from WAC, often in very different ways. We wanted the book to be full of faculty voices.

We adopted, therefore, the theoretical view of faculty that Hargreaves articulates and that we quoted at length on page 11 (this volume)—the view of faculty as active makers of meaning, as self-directed managers of their own change.

Refining the Research Questions

Within that frame, we articulated for this book five research questions that we thought our data would allow us to address—questions which were important to us as researchers and WAC directors and which, we thought, would be important to our readers:

1. What did faculty expect to gain from WAC?
2. What have their WAC experiences meant to them?
3. How did WAC influence their teaching philosophies and attitudes?
4. How did WAC influence their teaching strategies?
5. How did WAC influence their career patterns?

The Issue of Cause and Effect

The last three research questions raise the question of "influence." We have stated them that way because they were the questions that drove much of our data gathering and because they are the questions that, within the political contexts of most WAC programs, people want to ask and WAC programs try to answer. Constable aptly states our dilemma:

> All researchers know that to detect and record change is not the same thing as to identify the forces causing change. This knowledge is of little relief when the question of greatest interest is indeed 'What causes what?'. . . What is wanted is knowledge of whether initiatives have had the effects intended, but experience tells us that the questions are unlikely to be so simple in practice. (1994, 5)

Our data on "influences" largely (but not totally) relied upon asking faculty about WAC's effect on them. We generally asked our questions in rich contexts—interviews, small-group discussions—often gathering several types of data at several points over time from the same faculty member. These richly contextualized self-reports are valuable data to us because of our respect for the faculty member as a constructor of meaning and our interest in the faculty member's reasons, contexts, and growth. Who better than the faculty member, we reasoned, could tell us whether a particular change was motivated or influenced by what she or he heard in WAC?

But we did not rely entirely upon self-reports. Often, our interviews and small groups were accompanied by syllabi, assignment sheets, and other materials that provided evidence of the changes the faculty member described. Frequently, assignments or teaching ideas had begun in the WAC workshops and small groups where, in most cases, we ourselves were present. We observed classrooms and queried students. These data, and our multiple contacts with faculty over time, helped us to trace the influences.

Defining the Population under Study

As we assessed our data, we decided to place the greatest emphasis upon the faculty who had entered WAC earliest because the long-run view was important to us. These populations are explained in Table 2.3 and discussed at greater length in our next chapter on the individual schools. This decision to concentrate on early joiners meant that our population would probably contain many of those faculty whom Rogers (1983) calls "early adopters" of "innovations." His research suggests that these faculty would be comfortable with risk, not afraid of change, and horizontally networked—that is, with many connections to other faculty across campus, not just within their own departments. "Middle adopters," the research indicates, are slower to take risks and more "vertically" networked—that is, they maintain connections primarily within their own departments. Our personal knowledge of the faculty affirms this view of them as a group, although, as the rest of the book will show, a number of them started in WAC while they were still young, new, or insecure, and they credit WAC with having helped them to build networks, confidence, and the ability to take risks.

We tried throughout to include women's voices, and they are represented out of proportion to their numbers in the faculties of the three schools. Astin (1993) suggests that women faculty and faculty representing diverse ethnic and racial backgrounds are more likely to be responsive to underprepared students and to use student-centered teaching approaches. Thus this book may reflect the faculty who, either through ethnic and gender socialization or through temperament, are most amenable to the student-centered approaches of WAC.

Gathering the 1993–1995 Collaborative Data

Once we had decided to collaborate, had assessed our past data, and were in the process of refining our research questions and defining our population, we collected interviews and faculty-authored accounts on each campus (see Table 2.3, Item 9; Appendix E). We chose a variety of faculty who, earlier data had indicated, would represent a wide range of responses to WAC. We used these 1993–1995 interviews and accounts, then, to seek diversity of viewpoint; to update our records on some faculty about whom we already had earlier data; to focus specifically on our research questions; to add a body of data that was gathered in a somewhat consistent manner across all three campuses; and to record faculty voices that could be quoted directly in the book. Forty-two faculty—twenty-two from UC, ten from TSU, and ten from Whitworth—gave us interviews or their own authored accounts. We want to emphasize that, in almost all cases, we had earlier data on these faculty, so the interviews were a culmination and an updating. Table 2.4 summarizes the characteristics of the forty-two faculty members.

Data Analysis

Our Methods of Data Analysis

Looking for Common Themes

We analyzed all our data, looking for common themes, by using Spradley (1979; 1980) as a guide. To triangulate by researcher, we examined separately each other's interviews and faculty-authored accounts and then compared our interpretations. At the University of Cincinnati, Slachman and Walvoord identified themes independently.

Contributing to this process were earlier data analyses we had undertaken independently. For example, McMahon at Towson State

Table 2.4. Characteristics of the 42 faculty studied through interviews and self-authored reports, 1993–1995

Tenured:	34	Tenure-track untenured:	3
Nontenure track:	5	Minority:	1
Female:	20	Four-year/Graduate colleges:	39
Two-year colleges of UC:	3		
Disciplines:		Disciplines:	
Natural Sciences:	4	Social Sciences/Business:	11
Math/Computers:	4	Humanities/Languages/Arts:	15
Education and other preprofessional:	8		

n = 22 UC faculty, 10 TSU faculty, 10 Whitworth faculty

had noted a strong "problem-solution" frame in analyzing her eighteen faculty accounts in the booklet she published in-house in 1991. That frame helped to shape our section on why faculty came to WAC.

We had little trouble combining our themes; they were remarkably consistent. We further defined them through collaboration on multiple drafts of this book.

Including Dissident Voices

We tried to make the data analysis trustworthy by seeking out voices which did not fit the dominant themes that were emerging in the bulk of our data. We have included some of those voices in this book. Another way of assuring a range of voices was our large sample size. At Whitworth, we had multiple forms of data from virtually all of the faculty who attended workshops and then remained at Whitworth. At Cincinnati, we collected questionnaires and interviews from 89 percent (117) of the 131 faculty who had completed a two-day workshop between 1989 and 1991 and who were still on campus in 1991. We tracked down this 89 percent sample to try to ensure a wide variety of responses.

Challenges in Data Analysis

We struggled with several challenges throughout our data analysis. The first was the sheer variety of our data, collected under different circumstances, for different purposes, with different questions. We decided to rely most heavily on the final round of interviews and faculty accounts because they had been shaped for this study, they were somewhat consistent in method across the campuses, and they represented the most recent view. We also used heavily the published faculty accounts and the case studies that included classroom observations. These were the data where faculty spoke in their own voices, and we had their exact words. We used other data to enrich that material, to extend our data back into the past, to triangulate, and to suggest whom to interview in the final round to assure a range of WAC experiences.

Faculty self-reports posed several challenges. We value faculty self-reports because our focus is on how *faculty* make sense of their WAC experiences. These are not "weak" data to us in the same way as are the match-to-sample studies we summarized in the introduction. However, some problematic issues arose. First, asking questions specifically about WAC may have tended to highlight and foreground it from a mosaic where WAC might otherwise not have stood out in such bold relief. Faculty may have tended to give WAC too much credit for changes. Faculty may unconsciously have shaped their reports in the "conversion" or "testimonial" genre. On each campus, our research was directed from the WAC office, and in many cases the interviewer, while not the workshop leader, was the WAC director, a colleague well known to the faculty member. The impulse to please was undoubtedly present.

We countered these tendencies to highlight WAC and to please the WAC interviewer by:

- using a large sample size: trying to reach a large percentage of faculty;
- seeking out faculty who had different viewpoints about WAC;
- gathering data in various settings over time from the same faculty members;
- trying deliberately, in interviews, to bring out dissident points of view;
- examining syllabi and assignment sheets as part of interviews and faculty-authored presentations;
- observing classrooms;
- having the interview, in most cases, conducted by a person who had not led the WAC workshops the faculty member had attended, thereby giving the faculty member more freedom to be critical (Hunt interviewed at Whitworth, where

Walvoord had conducted workshops; Walvoord, Slachman, and Udel interviewed at Cincinnati, where workshops for the "Population A" faculty we studied most intensely [see Table 2.3] had been led by Fulwiler and Steffens; Dowling and McMahon interviewed at Towson State, where Dowling had led the Faculty Writers' Response Group and a few of the workshops, but where many workshops had been led by a number of others);

- talking with faculty in small groups, where faculty spoke before their peers and colleagues.

The small-group context was useful, we felt, because of the strong scholarly tradition of peer review, where faculty are accustomed to being held accountable for their words in a group of peers. Further, the tasks of the various small groups and committees—to conduct classroom research, to plan WAC activities, to respond to each other's writing or teaching plans—tended to bring out fuller data and to draw faculty away from testimonial presentations. The fact that many of the groups met over time and were informal meant that faculty answered unscripted questions about their classroom practices. Moreover, on each campus there were public presentations, both written and oral, by a number of our faculty to groups of their peers—groups that often included departmental colleagues who could evaluate the accuracy of the classroom procedures being described. Presenters responded to open questions from the audience. In virtually all of the public presentations, the teachers showed actual syllabi, assignment sheets, student work, or other documents.

The fact remains, however, that our data are better able to tell what faculty believe to have happened—and what WAC meant to them—than to pin down precisely what kinds of classroom changes actually happened in a scientifically verifiable way.

These, then, are our data and our methods for analyzing them. Throughout, we tried to listen to faculty and to understand their points of view. We believe that readers will find the voices that emerge in this book to be varied, rich, interesting, convincing in their candor, and fascinating in their various reflections on what WAC means to those who struggle daily in the classroom to find better ways of enhancing learning, creating community, and fulfilling the human spirit.

The next chapter presents in further detail each institution's characteristics, its WAC program, and its research data and methods.

3 Detailed Reports: The Institutions, Their WAC Programs, and Their Research Methods

UNIVERSITY OF CINCINNATI

by Barbara E. Walvoord, Virginia Slachman, and Lisa Udel

The University and Its WAC Program

The University of Cincinnati serves approximately 36,000 students in seventeen different, highly autonomous colleges, ranging from two-year to graduate-level colleges, and from open-admissions to highly selective. WAC began there in 1989 as part of a general education reform that would, for the first time, require a communications component in every general education course. Quickly expanding beyond general education to serve faculty as a whole, WAC, led by a strong faculty committee, enjoyed high visibility and success, as perceived by participants and administrators.

During the first two years, the program focused almost entirely on five two-day off-campus workshops, each with twenty to thirty full- and part-time faculty from a wide range of disciplines. Workshops were led by Toby Fulwiler and Henry Steffens from the University of Vermont and held in a restored Shaker village ("Shakertown") in rural Kentucky. The committee worked hard to attract highly influential faculty into the workshops. We will refer to this cohort of 1989–1991 Fulwiler-Steffens workshop faculty as "Population A," and our study follows them most closely (see Table 2.3).

In autumn 1991, Walvoord arrived to fill the newly created WAC director's position, and from that time until the end of this study, she led all the workshops herself—still two days and still at Shakertown. By 1995, 337 additional faculty had attended, and more were continually attending as the study developed. We will refer to these 1991–1995 Walvoord workshop faculty as "Population B."

After Walvoord's arrival, the WAC program grew rapidly and flourished. From 1991 to 1995, WAC offered a plethora of on-campus workshops ranging in duration from an hour to a day, as well as individual consultations. For example, during the academic year 1993–1994, WAC offered twenty-five on-campus workshops, three small groups of faculty working on classroom research, and numerous individual consultations, affecting, in all, 419 faculty who discussed WAC with Walvoord for more than half an hour (not all of them had attended the two-day workshop; thus not all are included in Population A or Population B).

WAC became a center of energy for the entire teaching-improvement emphasis at UC. WAC spawned a program to work with departmental cultures, which received a grant and established its own office, collaborating closely with WAC. WAC faculty were active in the many other teaching-enhancement initiatives springing up all across campus: ongoing plans for general education reform, oral and visual communication across the curriculum, critical thinking, math education reform, teaching workshops for engineers, assessment, Total Quality Management, and others. The WAC office organized a university-wide task force to construct a strategic plan for enhancing teaching and learning at UC. The WAC program was generously supported by top administrators, even through stringent budgetary cutbacks. The president began citing it widely in public as one of the stellar programs at the university. In the midst of running this growing and highly visible WAC program, then, we conducted our research on WAC outcomes.

Faculty Populations Studied

This account and our book focus most heavily on Population A—the 1989–1991 Fulwiler-Steffens workshop attendees—because they have the longest history. Also, Population A faculty, we reasoned, could be more candid with Walvoord, since she had not been present for their initial years in WAC. The 146 who originally attended a Fulwiler-Steffens workshop included full- and part-time faculty from a wide range of disciplines and at various levels, from instructor to full professor. In the academic year 1991–1992, when Walvoord arrived and began tracking them, 131 were still teaching at UC. During the following three years, we collected data from 117 of them. Thus we had data from 89 percent of those who had continued teaching at UC until 1991 (80 percent of the total 146 who had originally attended). Table 3.1 shows the characteristics of the 117 Population A faculty we contacted.

It must be remembered that Population A faculty were recruited by WAC Committee members who were themselves campus leaders and who specifically tried to tap other campus leaders. This recruitment, plus UC's sharp curtailment of new faculty tenure-track hires during the late 1980s, helps to account for the fact that our sample is 71 percent tenured (versus 54 percent of all UC full-time faculty, according to an editorial in the *Cincinnati Enquirer* of June 2, 1993). Moreover, it is possible that being tenured conferred upon faculty who came from four-year and graduate (and therefore more research-oriented) colleges a greater freedom to pay attention to teaching rather than research. We mentioned earlier that the WAC adherents at each college were "early adopters" and were thus perhaps distinguished by their willingness to take risks and by their horizontal networks across departmental lines.

We augmented Population A data with data from Population B, the 337 who had joined WAC from 1991 through 1995. Some members of Population B came to multidisciplinary workshops as part of a departmental cohort, or to discipline-specific workshops, which, we reasoned, would tend to encourage those "middle adopters" who tended to network more narrowly within their own departments. But we found essentially the same themes in Population B. The total of Populations A and B, 454 faculty, is about 25 percent of the full- and part-time UC faculty who teach undergraduates. It's possible that the 25 percent are still largely early adopters, or that the WAC workshops have had similar effects on early and middle adopters, or that the "adopter" research, which was conducted in fields other than teaching innovations, doesn't really fit the complex, multifaceted growth of a teacher.

Data Collection

Our data collection process followed the stages described in the next five sections.

Stage 1: Initial Population A Workshops, Follow-Up Lunches, and a Booklet of Faculty Writing

Before Walvoord arrived, five workshops had enrolled the Population A faculty, who had written responses to the workshops on the last day. A few follow-up luncheon sessions had been held on campus,

Table 3.1. Characteristics of the 117 UC Population A WAC faculty

Tenured:	71%	Tenure-track untenured:	11%
Nontenure track:	16%	Unknown:	2%
Female:	51%	Minority:	6%
Two-year colleges of UC:	23%	Four-year/Graduate colleges:	77%
Disciplines:		Disciplines:	
Natural Sciences:	10%	Social Sciences/Business:	18%
Math/Computers:	10%	Humanities/Languages/Arts:	32%
Education and other preprofessional:	30%		

where participants told of their experiences. No one took notes, but people later remembered some of what was said.

Also, in 1990, before Walvoord arrived, the WAC Committee published a booklet of essays and poems about teaching and learning, written by nineteen WAC workshop attendees.

Stage 2: The Initial Questionnaire/Interview, 1991–1992

Stage 2, 1991–1992, began shortly after Walvoord's arrival. Our methods were guided by two factors: as a new director, Walvoord needed to find out what had been happening, to get to know past WAC workshop attendees (Population A), and to tap their ideas for the future of the program. Further, since university resources were being sharply curtailed and public criticism of the university was rising, she was keenly aware of the need to demonstrate the program's success to administrators and external audiences in order to ensure continued funding and support.

To meet these needs, we (Walvoord and the graduate students who assisted in the WAC office for one year each and who co-authored this UC section of the study) focused on *change in teaching* as the measure of workshop success because it could easily be communicated to external audiences and was in line with the agenda of the public. Change remained a strong theme throughout all the UC data and in the final interviews collected on all three campuses for this book.

We gathered information on change through questionnaires that were combined with group and individual interviews and examinations of classroom assignments, syllabi, and similar documents. After a survey of questionnaires in the literature, we composed our own (Appendix C). The need for quick, easily comprehensible evidence of the program's "success" led us to ask faculty a few simple questions: "As a result of the Shakertown workshop, I have made at least some change in my teaching: Yes or No" and "The changes that I have made are . . . ." But our need for program planning and for getting to know these people led us to add several open-ended questions such as "Problems or questions that have arisen are . . . ."

In the first forty-three questionnaires, the question about what kinds of changes faculty had made was open-ended because we did not want to dictate the response options but rather to listen to what faculty said. We then used those forty-three answers to construct a set of stated options for the subsequent questionnaires (Appendix C shows these options). We stated the options because we wanted part of our sample to be responding to the same set of prompts so that we could compare the relative frequency of consistently worded responses.

Our need for more depth than a questionnaire could provide also led us to embed the questionnaires within small-group lunchtime discussions so that we could learn more. We invited all 131 Population A faculty who were then on campus. Eighty-four attended the luncheons in groups ranging from three to eight members. They filled out the questionnaire individually at the beginning, and then they discussed their WAC experiences and problems while Walvoord took notes.

We conducted telephone interviews with an additional seventeen faculty who did not attend discussions. Telephone responses were not substantially different from the discussion-group responses; frequently, telephoned faculty told us they had missed the small-group discussions simply owing to scheduling problems, not owing to disaffection. However, a few faculty appeared in this phone sample who had made little use of the workshop or who expressed disappointment in it. With one exception, every faculty member whom we were able to reach by phone agreed to be interviewed. Several others were away on sabbatical, and one person's husband refused to let us speak with her.

In Stage 2, then, we contacted 101 Population A faculty, which was 77 percent of the 131 who were still teaching on campus during 1991–1992. (In later stages we picked up an additional sixteen faculty for our total of 89 percent of the 131—see Tables 2.3 and 3.1.) Already, we were beginning to listen more richly and fully to faculty stories, rather than simply asking, "Did you change or didn't you?" or distributing a "match-to-sample" (page 3, this volume) questionnaire based on researchers' definitions of WAC strategies.

Stage 3: Small Discussion Groups, Faculty-Authored Accounts, Ethnographic Studies of Departmental Cultures, and a Classroom Case Study, 1992–1994

During the next two academic years, 1992–1994, we contacted fifty-seven of the 131 Population A faculty. About one-third of them were contacted two or more times. Sixteen of the fifty-seven had been missed in our 101 questionnaires of 1991–1992. Thus, within Stages 2 and 3 combined, we contacted 117 (89 percent) of the 131 Population A faculty (see Tables 2.3 and 3.1).

In Stage 3, we gathered data from small discussion groups of various kinds, from faculty-authored presentations or written articles, from ethnographic studies of departmental cultures, and from a classroom case study. The following numbers will add up to more than fifty-seven because some faculty participated in more than one activity. Walvoord took notes as forty-three Population A faculty, mixed with twenty-three Population B faculty, discussed their WAC strategies and problems in ninety-minute luncheon meetings. Walvoord also took notes, or we had the written texts and handouts, when twenty-four Population A faculty gave oral presentations or authored articles about their use of WAC strategies for audiences of other faculty. Seven Population A faculty, together with four Population B faculty, joined in classroom research groups that met three to eight times during an academic year. Thirty-three Population A faculty, along with Population B faculty and faculty who had not attended WAC workshops, served with Walvoord on various committees and task forces whose work gave rise to revelations about how the faculty member had been affected by WAC. Some examples were the WAC Committee, as well as the committee that planned and led lunchtime discussions on teaching, the committee that worked with other faculty to prepare and approve course proposals for general education courses which had a writing-intensive component, and committees that worked within individual departments to improve teaching. Walvoord took notes at these meetings.

During 1993, Walvoord, with several collaborators, began to study how the cultures of eight UC departments impacted teaching. Walvoord and her collaborators or interviewees discussed teaching and departmental cultures, examined departmental and teaching documents, or attended departmental meetings. The study, more broadly, gave Walvoord a rich view of the departmental contexts in which WAC faculty worked.

In 1993–1994, Walvoord collaborated with John Bryan (Population B) to study Bryan's business writing class, using interviews with students, classroom observations, interviews and informal discussions during work sessions with Bryan, examination of documents, and classroom transcripts (Walvoord and Bryan 1995).

One classroom visitation by Walvoord was conducted at the faculty member's request.

These data gave Walvoord a fuller, more varied and detailed, longitudinal view of how fifty-seven Population A faculty and various Population B faculty were developing between 1992 and 1994.

Stage 4: Mailed Questionnaire to Random Sample of UC Faculty, 1993–1994

In order to get a notion of the changes that faculty in the general population, not just WAC faculty, were experiencing, during 1993–1994 we mailed a questionnaire (Appendix A) to a random 20 percent of the full-time and most stable types of part-time faculty at UC. We received 147 faculty responses—a 54 percent return. The questionnaire asked faculty whether, during the past two years, they had made any changes in their teaching which they believed had enhanced student learning. If they responded yes, we asked them to indicate from a list all of the kinds of changes they had made. The list was composed of items that the research literature indicated to be productive of student learning (e.g., Chickering and Gamson 1987; for a discussion of measuring teacher behaviors to assess student learning, see National Center for Education Statistics 1995).

Stage 5: Interviews for This Book, 1993–1995

During 1993–1995, as we explained earlier, the book's co-authors collected interviews and faculty-authored accounts on all three campuses, specifically for this book. At UC, we did twenty-two interviews with Population A faculty, deliberately trying to include some who had varying reactions to WAC. All interviews were taped and transcribed. Slachman conducted twelve of the interviews, drawing on her experience as a professional journalist and writer and going over her interview techniques with Walvoord as they reviewed her first few interview tapes. Five of the interviews were conducted by graduate students from Walvoord's "Research Methods in Composition" class. Three other faculty contacted by the graduate students declined to be interviewed, citing time constraints or not having used WAC strategies. Walvoord conducted five interviews.

The interviews were semistructured—that is, the interviewer tried to cover a list of questions (Appendix E) but not in any particular order, and the researcher used interviewee responses as the basis for further questions.

The UC interviewees quite closely resemble the Population A faculty profiled in Table 3.1, except that the interviewees included 20 percent natural science faculty and only 10 percent education and pre-professional faculty.

The quoted statements from UC faculty in this book are derived mainly from these last twenty-two interviews because these provided the most long-range and recent data. We also drew upon all the other data we had collected, including our often numerous, previous contacts with these same faculty.

In addition to the questionnaires, interviews, and discussion groups with WAC participants and the random questionnaire to UC faculty in general, we also, for this study, drew upon Walvoord's myriad informal contacts with WAC participants at UC between 1991 and 1995. At meetings, social occasions, or campus walks, people would come up and describe the latest things they were doing. Walvoord also periodically made dozens of "cold calls" to faculty listed in the campus phone directory, inviting them to workshops. These calls elicited their responses as well as stories they had heard from others. The specific data we have mentioned, then, were embedded in a rich anecdotal fund of information about what WAC participants were doing—information that proved consistent with what we heard in the more formal types of data.

TOWSON STATE UNIVERSITY

by H. Fil Dowling Jr., Joan D. McMahon, and Barbara E. Walvoord

The University and Its WAC Program

Towson State University, near Baltimore, has 15,000 students in its baccalaureate and master's programs. Towson has one of the earliest writing-intensive course requirements, instituted in 1976 when a revised curriculum requirement mandated that all students take a W-I course (usually elected in the student's major field). By 1994, forty-four different W-I courses in twenty-five departments were offered, taught by faculty in those departments. Most of these faculty were full-time tenured or tenure-track.

TSU's WAC activities have been interdisciplinary from the start. An Advanced Writing Course Committee, started in 1976 and commonly consisting of eight faculty members from five or six different disciplines, creates standards and guidelines for the W-I courses, evaluates and approves new W-I courses, and (since 1982) sponsors workshops and other faculty development activities. A coordinator of WAC (Dowling) chairs the Advanced Writing Course Subcommittee and helps implement its activities.

These activities were stimulated in 1981 when Towson joined the newly created Baltimore Area Consortium for Writing Across the Curriculum (BACWAC), which in turn launched the Maryland Writing Project (MWP), affiliated with the National Writing Project. MWP has been headquartered at Towson since 1984. TSU's WAC coordinator, Dowling, attended MWP's first five-week Summer Institute in 1981 and has played a leadership role in BACWAC (See Walvoord and Dowling 1990). Many other Towson faculty have been involved in WAC training offered by those two groups. A variety of other campus activities have influenced Towson's WAC teachers, among them a series of workshops funded by the Fund for the Improvement of Post-Secondary Education (FIPSE) during 1985–1987 to mainstream women's studies into Towson's regular curriculum, including W-I courses; a Center for the Teaching and Study of Writing, established in 1989; and the faculty development activities of McMahon (who earlier had attended and then co-led WAC workshops with Dowling), culminating in her 1994 appointment as project director for the University Teaching Initiative. Both Dowling and McMahon received released time to coordinate WAC activities.

Faculty Population Studied

The faculty population consisted of approximately 200 faculty who were involved in workshops, the Faculty Writers' Response Group, and other WAC activities on Towson's campus, in the BACWAC consortium, in the Maryland Writing Project, and at neighboring schools. Nearly 100 of the TSU faculty at any given time teach W-I courses.

Data Collection

Presentations by WAC Participants

Towson began its own series of WAC workshops in 1984, ranging from ninety minutes to two days long and led by members of its own faculty. The two-day workshops present a concise but detailed guide to WAC theory and practice, including assignment planning, writing-to-learn, syllabus revision, handling peer-response groups, evaluation of writing, and helpful auxiliary services (such as the Student Writing Lab).

The workshops encourage active learning: participants write through-out the workshop and develop at least one practical item, such as a writing assignment, that can be used immediately in their W-I courses. These two-day workshops are supplemented by ninety-minute work-shops, also led by TSU faculty from a range of disciplines. They focus on a single ingredient of WAC teaching, such as developing effective ways of responding to and evaluating student writing, combating students' basic writing problems, or organizing effective student-response groups. These faculty presentations were one source of data at Towson.

Classroom Observations

One of the richest sources of data at Towson (and an activity that our data indicate had a strong impact on participating faculty) was the individual, one-on-one, intensive work that Dowling did with twenty-one faculty between 1982 and 1994. At the invitation of the faculty member, Dowling attended a class for three to four weeks, talking with students and consulting with the teacher on curriculum, assignments, methods, and evaluation of writing. Not an evaluator of the visited courses, Dowling simply tried to serve as an equal and non-threatening colleague who happened to be informed about writing theory and practice. Through this classroom observation, Dowling was able to observe and compare techniques used by the WAC faculty, including methods presented to those teachers in workshops, and to observe the faculty members' thinking and approach to WAC.

Observations of Faculty in Groups

The Faculty Writers' Response Group, with a membership of ten to twenty at any given time, has involved at least forty different teachers since its inception in 1985. The group provides a supportive environment for faculty to work on their own writing by acting as a peer-response group for faculty drafts. It also models WAC concepts such as writing-to-learn, the writing process, and response groups, which faculty can then use in their own teaching. Dowling has been a member since 1985, observing how faculty use workshop-suggested techniques within both the group and their own classrooms and how they have grown and developed over time.

Case Study of a Biology Classroom

Between 1983 and 1986, Anderson, a TSU biologist who had attended WAC workshops, and Walvoord conducted a naturalistic study of one of Anderson's courses, an upper-level W-I course, during three different semesters. During the three years, Anderson significantly changed the way she taught the course. The study focused on the difficulties that students encountered, the new teaching strategies that Anderson used, and the subsequent differences in student work on the assignment. Published in 1991 (Anderson and Walvoord), it provided a rich, deeply contextualized view of a WAC teacher's growth over time.

McMahon's Interviews

In 1991, McMahon, using a sabbatical, interviewed eighteen Towson WAC teachers about their use of writing in their courses and published an in-house booklet in which they described their theories, methods, and problem-solutions for teaching writing.

Workshop Evaluation Data

We had evaluation data collected from ninety-eight faculty at the conclusion of six of Towson's in-house WAC workshops between 1984 and 1989.

Interviews for This Book

After this book project began, during 1993–1995, Dowling and McMahon conducted, taped, and transcribed interviews with five active WAC faculty at Towson (questions, Appendix E) and solicited narratives from five other WAC faculty who described the impact WAC had on them. Most of these faculty narratives were read and discussed by the Faculty Writers' Response Group and then revised.

WHITWORTH COLLEGE

by Linda Lawrence Hunt

The College and Its WAC Program

Whitworth College, a private, liberal arts, Presbyterian-related college in Spokane, Washington, has about 2,000 students. The increasingly selective undergraduate population of 1,400 has an entering grade-point average of 3.5; there are master's programs in education, music, and international management.

WAC began at Whitworth in 1987, when the Faculty Assembly voted to require a writing-intensive course in the major, after many faculty expressed frustration with their students' lack of writing skills.

The director of Composition (Linda Hunt) and the assistant to the Provost (Tammy Reid—a former English faculty member and now Acting Dean of the Faculty) co-authored a grant for a two-year faculty development program funded by CAPHE (Consortium for the Advancement of Private Higher Education) and the M. J. Murdock Charitable Trust. This faculty administration cooperative spirit has permeated WAC efforts at Whitworth.

The primary emphasis has been a series of three- to five-day writing workshops led by Barbara Walvoord and augmented by in-house consultants and faculty presentations. Twenty-six faculty (about one-third of the total faculty) volunteered in May of 1989 for the initial five-day workshop, held on campus. The topics included connecting course goals with types of writing assignments, designing effective assignments, peer editing and faculty conferencing on rough drafts, revising, managing grammar and usage, and reallocating faculty time evaluating papers. Each faculty member chose one class to redesign. Faculty brought their new course syllabi or writing assignments to colleagues for response. For most faculty, this was the first time they had had a chance to hear faculty outside their departments talk in depth about their goals and enthusiasm for their discipline. Often, it was also the first time they had experienced peer response on course assignments. Written evaluations of the workshops were very positive.

In the fall of 1989, Whitworth dedicated an entire faculty development day to WAC, led by William Zinsser. The following May, twenty faculty volunteered for the second Faculty Writing Workshop, a four-day event. Twelve faculty who had been through the previous workshop also returned for a two-day advanced workshop. These were led by Walvoord, with Hunt and Reid acting as consultants. The advanced workshop focused on critical-thinking skills. Considerable time was given to faculty reports on what was working and what was still troublesome. Also, Walvoord held individual conferences with faculty to discuss specific syllabi, assignments, or general frustration.

By 1991, sixty-six faculty (over three-fourths of the total faculty) had experienced some version of a writing workshop. The general response remained very positive. Several faculty wrote in their self-evaluations for promotion and tenure about the specific ways these workshops had shaped their classroom teaching.

Since the completion of the grant, Whitworth has offered further in-house workshops for new faculty and veterans each year. These workshops are generally co-directed by Hunt and Reid, with faculty serving as primary resources.

In the spring of 1991, Whitworth sponsored two in-house workshops designed by Hunt and Reid. One was for faculty who had missed the earlier two workshops. Five previous faculty workshop attendees, who represented a range of disciplines, presented the changes they had made and showed the impact of those changes upon the learning in their classes.

Another "follow-up" workshop was an afternoon/dinner/ evening meeting for fifteen faculty in a conference room at a Spokane hotel. Again, the focus was on "What's working, and where do you want more help?" Several faculty spoke of the exciting responses they'd received from students about their new assignments.

In the fall of 1994, with a smaller grant from Washington Trust matched by institutional support, Walvoord returned for two days of workshops. On the first day, fourteen new faculty were introduced to WAC, and on the second day, a follow-up was held for twelve faculty, in which considerable time was given for them to report their WAC experiences. In 1995 and 1996, Walvoord again led workshops.

When Whitworth began its WAC program, there was no Writing Center on campus, a critical support component if writing-intensive courses are required. By 1991, a center was begun in the new library with leadership provided by Marty Erb, a member of the composition faculty. From the inception, it was intentionally designed for all students, not just those perceived as needing "remedial" support. The center was staffed primarily by trained student writing consultants; however, from the beginning, several faculty volunteered to be consultants by holding one of their traditional office hours in the Writing Center instead of their offices. This has provided faculty with an ongoing awareness of how students perceive writing assignments, what difficulties they encounter, and what specific suggestions prove helpful. Students also bring in graduate school and scholarship applications for which faculty can be a prime resource. This program has continued as a distinctive component of Whitworth's WAC emphasis.

Data Collection

Interviews with Faculty

In 1990–1991, Hunt interviewed twelve faculty from a range of disciplines to learn what was working and also where faculty felt frustrated. She also met with student TAs in the psychology program. The primary purpose of these interviews was to allow faculty to discuss their experiences and to offer assistance with specific issues (for example, how to work with large classes, or strategies for effective conferencing). Another important purpose was to help design each new workshop.

Observation of Faculty CORE Teams

All students at Whitworth take three required CORE ("core curriculum") courses which are team taught and must have a writing component. The CORE teams work together closely to plan the course and the assignments. This interchange, in which Hunt participates, has given faculty intimate acquaintance with each other's pedagogical and philosophical thinking and growth over the years. The teamwork also supported that growth. As she led the workshops, Walvoord found the coherence within teams to be a unique characteristic that set Whitworth faculty apart from those in other workshops she had led, even at small schools. In 1990–1991, Hunt met with the four-person faculty team that was teaching one of the CORE courses. Over the years, she observed five additional CORE faculty in teams of which she was a member.

Faculty Presentations

Throughout the WAC program, faculty have frequently been called on to give reports on their classroom experiences to other faculty colleagues. In the second year of the grant, for instance, six faculty presentations included conferencing methods, writing research papers, designing new assignments, helping students with lab reports, and connecting goals to writing projects. Faculty talked about both satisfying and frustrating experiences, since one goal of the grant committee was to create a climate of trust, where faculty could be honest about both the positive and negative dimensions of attempting changes in their teaching. Hunt and Reid took notes on faculty feedback.

Student Questionnaires and Interviews

Throughout the initial two-year grant period, 1989–1991, student-response sheets gave quantifiable feedback for faculty at the end of writing-intensive courses and CORE courses (which had a required writing component). During four semesters, 1,157 students responded to a short questionnaire (Appendix D) on the writing component of the class, which assessed their attitudes toward rewriting papers, learning course material through writing assignments, clarity of the writing instruction, effectiveness of faculty-student conferencing, and their improvement as writers. These were shared with faculty members.

In the spring of 1991, student consultants from the Writing Center interviewed a random group of sixteen juniors and seniors who had been through the CORE courses and writing-intensive classes. These taped thirty- to forty-five-minute interviews with their peers provided a candid glimpse of how students perceived Whitworth's increased emphasis on writing. They also provided an insightful critique concerning the help students needed from faculty. These interviews were transcribed and communicated, in summary, to faculty through the WAC booklet described below.

The Writing-Across-the-Curriculum Booklet

By the end of the two-year grant period, Whitworth faculty had reported so many significant changes in their classroom teaching that the college wanted to ensure that the WAC program would continue. One effort was the 1992 in-house publication of *Writing Across the Curriculum*, a 113-page booklet which showcased eleven faculty-authored stories. Faculty reports followed a common pattern: first, faculty's initial classroom experience with writing which motivated their participation in the workshops; then, the specific changes they had made in one class after the workshop; and finally, the results of these changes, both positive and negative. They also included assignment sheets or syllabi which demonstrated these changes. The purpose of the stories and sample assignments was to provide models for other faculty, including new faculty, who would be teaching writing-intensive classes. The booklet also included a history of the grant, campus goals, writing-intensive course requirements, W-I course lists, handouts from Walvoord's workshops, student-feedback sheets which faculty could "lift," and summaries from the student questionnaires and interviews. This booklet was given to each faculty member and to all new faculty during their orientation at Whitworth. It also was offered as a resource to other colleges. An enthusiastic review of the booklet in a CAPHE publication led to inquiries from sixteen to twenty other small liberal arts colleges across the country.

Final Round of Interviews for This Book

Ten faculty, representing a broad range of disciplines, were interviewed by Hunt in 1994 (questions, Appendix E). These forty- to fifty-minute interviews were taped, transcribed, analyzed, and shared with the other researchers working on this book.

Witworth College Faculty Survey

In the spring of 1995, the Whitworth Faculty Writing Committee decided it was time to survey all faculty teaching Writing-Intensive (W-designated) courses. The undergraduate enrollment had been climbing steadily in the past two years without an equal growth in additional faculty; consequently, this was affecting aspects of the WAC program, particularly class size in some of the W-designated courses. We also wanted data on the types of assignments, various approaches to writing objectives, options offered for revision within each major, the use and usefulness of peer and/or faculty conferences, and feedback on additional support faculty wanted and needed.

The response was excellent. Thirty-eight faculty, representing fifty-five classes, answered the two-page, open-ended questionnaire, almost an 80 percent return rate. This provided significant information to the Writing Committee, which has been useful in planning strategies and programs to address faculty concerns. It also provided encouragement on the value faculty place in the use of W-courses in the majors.

4 What Did Faculty Expect from WAC?

I have this compulsion to keep trying to make my teaching better.
—Art History, Whitworth

You don't have to be a convert.
—Architecture, UC

In our final round of 1993–1995 interviews on all three campuses, we asked faculty to recall why they had come to the WAC events they had attended four, ten, sometimes fifteen years earlier. What did they want and expect from WAC? Our end-of-workshop faculty responses throughout the years and McMahon's interviews for the booklet at Towson likewise address that issue.

Faculty reported that they did not come to WAC in a vacuum. Rather, they came with already formed goals and problems which they were working on or because they appreciated the need for periodic reflection and renewal.

Further, they saw the workshop as part of an ongoing pattern of change in their teaching—change which they themselves controlled and directed. They assumed the right to adopt or adapt whatever in WAC was useful to them and to abandon or ignore whatever was not. They assumed that they would continue to change and grow after WAC, just as they had been changing prior to WAC. They did not see themselves as passive recipients of WAC, nor as static or sinning or sick before WAC. To them, WAC was a resource, not a religion. Its purpose was to help them with their own journey.

> *Faculty members' image of themselves as self-directed managers of their own continual change and growth underlies everything else in this book.*

Faculty Came to WAC for Help with Already Formed Problems and Goals

A UC geographer stopped the interviewer early in the session to say, "You need to understand why I went to the workshop in the first place." He then described the problems he had been wrestling with five years earlier, when he had attended his first WAC workshop. Joan McMahon, in 1988, was so struck by the problem orientation in the eighteen TSU faculty she interviewed that she organized her book (McMahon 1991) around it: in that book, each faculty member describes a teaching problem and the way he or she tried to address it. That problem orientation was strong, as well, in our data at all three institutions.

What types of goals and problems did faculty report? The best answer is *a very wide variety.* But common themes appeared, such as the following:

- enhancing students' higher-order thinking or habits of mind;
- making students more active learners;
- evaluating student work more effectively.

Faculty interviews were often marked by goals that formed a kind of touchstone for each faculty member's thinking and teaching. "I wanted my students to link their lives to the content" was the theme that appeared again and again when we interviewed a UC sociologist. A Whitworth musician told us, "What I've always tried to do at Whitworth is teach openness." A mathematician, just before he came to the WAC workshop at UC, had been assigned to teach a math course for nonmajors, and he came with general goals for that course already worked out:

> Independent of any knowledge about WAC, I wanted the course to have an, I don't know what to call it exactly, an expository feel to it—here are the ideas, here's why we care about the ideas—rather than computations.

Problems which participants mentioned included specific teaching challenges, constraints that were hindering the realization of goals, or a sense that what they were doing wasn't working.

Below is a sample of faculty voices from our 1993–1995 interviews at all three schools.

"I Had Always Used Writing, but I Teach Large Classes"
—Geography, UC

My major problem and the thing that drove me to the workshop is that I teach large classes—180–220 students. In part because I come out of a history tradition and in part because of where I did my doctorate, I have always used writing in my classes regardless of the size. But with 180–220 students, it was not only time-consuming, but I was the laughing stock of my department because I was spending an inordinate amount of time grading. Even if I didn't correct the grammar and spelling and syntax, I felt obligated to do a little rewriting, to tell the students what I felt were the strong points, the weak points. Now people would say, "Sure it's possible with smaller classes, but with classes of 220 you give multiple-choice exams and that's it, who cares, let 'em be." So I really wanted either to find other people who were doing what I was so I wouldn't feel like a fool or to find out some tricks.

"I Was Trying to Get Students Just to Think"
—Criminal Justice, UC

I was sort of doing some of these writing things, but I didn't know there was a whole pedagogy or ideology until I went to the workshop. I was trying to do different things with formal and informal writing, trying to get students just to think about what they were doing, also trying to make sure they were doing the reading, trying to think of ways to improve their writing that would not be terribly time-consuming for me. It was very much by the seat of my pants.

"I Was Already in the Throes of Planning
What to Do with 'Topics in Math'"
—Math, UC

The writing-across-the-curriculum workshop came to my attention just as I was in the midst of planning change. Up until the time I took part in the workshop, I had taught courses aimed at the engineering students and graduate courses—fairly hard-core traditional math courses. In the winter of 1990, I was asked to start planning to take over in the fall of '90 a course called "Topics in Math," which is a course for people who don't want to take math, people in arts and sciences. The book we had selected was very much mathematics as an appreciation subject, rather than as a subject for building technical skills. So I was already in the throes of planning how to teach such a course when I went to the workshop. So WAC, for me, was always thought of in those terms—what am I going to do with it in "Topics in Math."

"Students Were Not Achieving"
—Health Science and Human Resources, TSU

[Before WAC] I had begun to wonder why my students were getting C's. I noticed how hard they worked and how frustrated they appeared with their grades. Gradually, I began to focus on why they weren't achieving. I saw this initially as a learning problem, which eventually led me to the fact that it was a teaching problem. . . . I began to investigate other ways I could learn to improve my students' writing.

"When You Land at Whitworth after a Large University, You Find That Lecture-Oriented Teaching Doesn't Work Here"
—Sociology, Whitworth

I had come back to Whitworth after teaching at a large university where I taught mostly large classes. So I had cultivated a very lecture-oriented teaching style. And when you land at Whitworth, it doesn't take long to figure out that that doesn't work here. To me, it was a faculty development process of learning some new and better ways of teaching.

"Correcting Students' Mistakes Wasn't Getting Me Anywhere"
—History, Whitworth

Before the workshop, I'd always felt strongly about writing and I'd always been a stickler for grammar and punctuation. I could correct mistakes, and I always did, but it didn't get me anywhere. It didn't help the students. And I'd try to figure out how to do that better. The only agenda I had was just to know different ways, more effective ways, to do this. . . . And also maybe different ways to craft assignments, too, because I'm always looking for that.

———

Faculty Came to WAC for Renewal

A second reason faculty gave for entering WAC was personal renewal or development of their own skills, energy, or commitment. Below is a sample, beginning with a Towson faculty member who entered not a workshop, but a Faculty Writers' Response Group whose purpose was to respond to faculty members' own writings. The final two entries are divergent voices that don't fit either of our two reasons.

"I Joined to Become a Better Writer"
—Speech and Mass Communications, TSU

I joined the Faculty Writers' Response Group primarily to become a better writer. I had embarked on one of the most important writing projects of my life: the first textbook in my field to address in depth the ethical issues involved in managing public relations campaigns. As a man who likes long-distance running and has run a few marathons, I knew the value of discipline and training. I knew that working on a regular basis with the Faculty Writers' Response Group would provide me with an intellectual arena, with supporters along the sidelines to goad me so that I would pace myself appropriately through the process of writing a 475-page book. . . . What I didn't expect from the Faculty Writers' Response Group was learning not only how to become a better writer, but also how to become a better teacher.

"When Whitworth Does Something, You'd Better Get In on It"
—Music, Whitworth

I always take advantage of workshops that Whitworth provides. I'm very, very busy, and chairing the department, and I have a lot of things going on in my profession. But Whitworth can't do a lot, and when it does something, you'd better get in on it. . . . I must show my students that I am availing myself of opportunities as I want them to avail themselves of things we offer.

"When I See Workshops Advertised, I'm One of the First to Sign Up"
—Nursing, TSU

Interviewer: Tell me how you got involved with the writing-across-the-curriculum movement?

Faculty: There were some workshops on campus by Fil Dowling. When I see workshops advertised on campus by another department, if they at all relate to what we're doing, I'm one of the first to sign up, just because I want to know more about whatever the topic is. There were probably six of us in the department who went to that workshop, and as we talked about it, we got excited about it.

"You've Got to Hook Up with Other People"
—Political Science, UC

It's a big struggle to match your teaching strategies to the philosophy you really believe in. That's if you don't get so discouraged that you give up on those philosophies or change them and decide that students aren't learning or can't. You have to hook up with other people and share their philoso-phies—people who are struggling against the same realities that you are. I think you have to affirm to each other that these things are important. Without that support, you can feel very isolated and discouraged. That was part of my motivation for going to the workshop.

Divergent Voices

"I Was Looking for Anything That Offered Released Time"
—Biology, TSU

I would love to tell you that it was great insight on my part or great recruit-ment by the WAC movement that led me to the workshop, but it wasn't. I was mother to two teenagers, teaching twelve hours, over forty, and thrilled-to-death pregnant. As fall classes started, I was looking for anything that offered released time, and the WAC project promised it.

"Uh, I Don't Remember. Did It Have Any Money Involved?"
—Whitworth

[From an interview five years after the workshop:]

Interviewer: Why did you go to the workshop?

Faculty: Uh, I don't remember. Did it have any money involved? (laughter)

Mixed Reasons—Social, Idealistic, Practical

A variety of other motivations for workshop attendance turned up, and, of course, a single person might have several motives. At UC, one difference between Population A faculty, who were the first on campus to attend the WAC workshops, and Population B, who attended in later years (see Table 2.3), is that Population B, at the beginning of the workshops, more often cited colleague testimonials as a motivation for their own attendance. This same social motivation turned up in one of our TSU interviewees, a physical education faculty member, whose words also show a mixture of social, idealistic, and practical motives. She begins, "My colleague encouraged me to go." Another factor was her already formed philosophy of teaching: "I believed in required writing assignments." And then there was a very practical reason: the writing-intensive requirement "more or less ensured a full class as a hedge against the vagaries of fluctuating student numbers."

Undoubtedly, then, there were a number of factors that accounted for faculty members' entrance into WAC. But among the most commonly mentioned in our data were faculty members' already formulated goals and problems and their recognition of their need for periodic renewal.

Faculty Expected WAC to Be Part of Their Self-Directed Change and Growth

In faculty members' eyes, the problems and goals that motivated them to come to WAC writing groups or workshops were not static states—nor were they beginning points in the teaching journey. Rather, those problems and goals were part of what faculty saw as a career-long pattern of constant growth and change—a pattern that had begun before WAC and would continue after it. "I learned to be a nurse years and years ago," said a nursing faculty member from TSU, "but I learned to be a teacher along the way, and I think that learning continues. Hardly a semester goes by that I don't learn something new." Problems, setbacks, distractions, stall-outs, and dead ends were seen as temporary limitations to this impetus for change and improvement.

Interviewer: *"Did you change your teaching because of WAC?"*

Faculty: *"I just kind of change my assignments all the time."*

— History, Raymond Walters College of UC (2-year, open-admissions)

"I experiment and change all the time. I'll try anything that works."

—International Business, TSU

UC's survey of a random sample of faculty—not just those who had attended WAC—showed this sense of constant change to be widespread. Of the 147 UC faculty responses (a 54 percent return), 90 percent reported having, in the past twelve months, "made a change in my undergraduate teaching intended to result in enhanced student learning" (Table 4.1). In an essay on researching classroom change,

Table 4.1. UC faculty's self-reported changes in teaching

Responders	Method	Results
117 UC Population A WAC faculty 6–24 months after WAC workshop. (117 = 89% of the total 1989–1991 Population A attendees who were still on campus in 1991. See p. 36 and Table 2.3 for further details.)	Questionnaire with interview and/or small-group discussion (Appendix C).	99% reported having changed teaching as a result of workshop.
147 UC faculty from random sample. (Random sample was 20% of all faculty. 147 = 54% return. See p. 39 and Table 2.3 for further details.)	Mailed questionnaire (Appendix A).	90% reported having, in the past 12 months, changed their teaching to enhance student learning.

Constable notes that "change does not either happen or not happen. It is rare for nothing to happen" (1994, 5). Given that faculty in our *general* UC sample saw themselves as changing constantly, it is not surprising that *WAC faculty, too,* saw themselves as always changing and that 99 percent of our 117-person UC Population A WAC sample reported having made at least some change in their teaching as a result of the WAC workshop.

Self-reports are questionable evidence when one is trying to measure the amount of change that actually took place. But our point here is different. Our data indicate that faculty outside of WAC as well as in WAC *see themselves* as constantly changing. WAC directors and others who hope to help them change must deal with these self-perceptions.

The literature on faculty vitality we cited in the introduction (page 5, this volume) indicates that change and the seizing of opportunity are part of faculty vitality. Further, if the faculty in WAC workshops fit the characteristics we summarized for "early adopters," then continual change and the willingness to take risks are common traits. We earlier suggested that WAC faculty, on the whole, are both "vital" and "early adopters."

Stimuli to Faculty Change

What stimulated faculty change? Often, faculty reported that changes in their teaching were goal-driven, aimed at specific problems or concerns. But change might also follow a new stimulus—a workshop, hearing a good idea from a colleague, reading something.

Also, sometimes change occurred just because of the constant change process. Faculty felt themselves immersed in an ongoing river of change, moving constantly into new teaching strategies, even leaving behind strategies that had worked well in the past. An art historian at Whitworth mused:

> I did the peer editing, maybe six years ago. I might try that again. [Pause] I haven't thought about that in a long time. I'd sort of forgotten about doing that. Um hm. [Pause] Well, I keep rewriting my syllabus every year and changing assignments. It's not so much that they don't work; it's just that I have this compulsion to keep trying to make them better.

Changes in teaching sometimes also occurred serendipitously. One faculty member we interviewed reported he kept a log from semester to semester, noting things that had worked, things that had not, and things he had changed. He consulted the log whenever he was making up the syllabus for the next semester. But it was rare to find planning so organized. Many faculty reflected a looser, more serendipitous mode, incorporating things they had been newly exposed to or things they were thinking about at the time. Not teaching a course for a long period of time or having many courses to think about simultaneously might cause a more disrupted planning flow. Sometimes teaching strategies would be forgotten or drop away by default. Musing about why he had changed from required draft conferences, which replaced one week's class sessions, to voluntary ones, which did not replace class, a Whitworth political scientist said,

> Well, it probably was a conscious decision to put back the week of missed classes. Or maybe it's just that I didn't think about it when I was redoing the syllabus. I'm not a person who always plans everything down to the last minute.

Some faculty on all three campuses credited the WAC programs with enhancing the pace of change or their willingness to change, as well as with giving them the freedom to direct their own patterns of change. A UC geographer said: "I imagine that, at some point, the changes would have happened anyway; it's just that the workshop has probably accelerated them." An adjunct political scientist teaching in UC's evening college said: "The workshop made clear that some-body respected my intellect and assumed the best of me." Encouraged by that respect, she reported: "I'm willing to risk more. . . . My class-room has become the never-ending draft."

In sum, faculty took responsibility for managing their own growth and change. They did not see themselves as converts or resisters to WAC but as self-directed seekers. WAC was a resource, not a religion. They felt free to take what they needed, combine it with other things, and make their own unique mix, which itself would continue to change. "You don't have to be a convert," said a UC professor of architecture.

We suggest that WAC pro-grams must not cling to models which subtly assume that the faculty member changes in the WAC workshop and then does not change again, or that the only "acceptable" change is change in the direction of "full implementation" of WAC-defined classroom paradigms (page 6, this volume). Our data suggest that continual change, or at least their own perception of continual change, is a central characteristic of many WAC fac-ulty. WAC programs must deal with faculty members' continual change as a fundamental and desirable characteristic and must grant to faculty the right and the encouragement to direct their own growth and change both inside and outside of WAC.

> *"One impact the workshop had on me was making me feel more secure about trying some of the different creative things or coming up with new things. And also deciding that it was OK if they flopped."*
>
> —Criminal Justice, UC

> *"It varies, whatever I feel like doing. But mainly, since the workshop, I just feel more apt to try something if I think of it. It encourages you to experiment with things."*
>
> —Chemistry, UC

Faculty came into WAC workshops, faculty response groups, and other activities seeking help with their own problems and goals, immersing themselves in a river of change, and actively seeking to manage that change for their own growth as teachers. What those WAC experiences meant to them is the subject of the next chapter.

5 What Did WAC Experiences Mean to Faculty?

There was an instant sense of community.
—Geography, UC

What did these faculty remember about WAC groups and workshops after two, five, ten, in some cases fifteen years? In a word, they remembered *community*. Their perception of that community shaped how they would later remember and use their WAC experiences. For most of them, the community experience in WAC had been energizing and instructive. They reported using it as a model for their own teaching and their own collegial relationships. And some extended the WAC community across time and across boundaries, weaving a connective web of relationships that both sustained and supported their teaching and their further growth. In contrast, a few remembered disruptions to the community they sought.

Our interviews and faculty-authored accounts collected on all campuses across the years, and especially in 1993–1995, were our main data sources for this chapter.

WAC Programs: A Brief Description

In order to understand faculty members' recollections, we need to describe the workshops and groups our interviewees attended at the three schools. All three institutions have continued to hold workshops and other activities, but since our long-range study concentrates on faculty who attended the early activities, this description focuses on those.

At UC and Whitworth, the early experiences were workshops of two to five days, held in a peaceful setting on or off campus, each attended by fifteen to thirty interdisciplinary faculty. Especially notable is the setting for UC's workshops—a restored Shaker village in the rolling, green hills of rural Kentucky. There the religious society called "Shakers" lived and worked, sharing all goods in common, striving to create a visionary society of God, and constructing the strong and simple buildings, tools, quilts, and furniture among which the workshop participants ate, slept, and talked for two days. It is not insignificant that at UC the workshops were almost universally referred to not as "the workshop" but as "Shakertown"—a clue, perhaps, to the impact of this visionary community upon the communities that formed within the workshops themselves.

At UC during 1989–1991, before Walvoord's arrival, Toby Fulwiler and Henry Steffens of the University of Vermont used the methods described in Fulwiler's "Showing, Not Telling, at a Writing Workshop" (1981). The workshop typically had twenty-five to thirty faculty, many of whom did not know one another. The Fulwiler-Steffens workshops stressed journals and other types of informal writing, peer collaboration, and guiding of the writing process, including draft responses. The two-day sessions began with workshop attendees reading Scudder's account (see Bean 1992), in which he describes how a professor made him *look* at a fish for hours on end. Participants wrote responses to this article, often wonderfully imaginative and thoughtful ones. They shared them in groups, revised, wrote responses in a different vein, shared, and revised again. Small groups met, as well, to discuss various teaching problems raised among the participants. The idea was that, by writing themselves and sharing in small groups, participants would *experience,* not merely be told about, the power of writing for learning. The energy and commitment generated by the writing and small groups powered the production, by a volunteer group of faculty after the workshop, of an in-house booklet containing nineteen of these "Fish Stories."

At Whitworth, from 1989 to 1992, Walvoord ran workshops more like the one described by Herrington (1981), which began with learning goals and followed the course-planning process. Held from three to five days in a quiet room on campus, the workshops included twelve to fifteen faculty, all of whom, at this small school, knew one another. The workshop began by asking participants to define, in writing, the kinds of learning they wanted from their students in a particular class. That writing became the basis for pedagogical planning. Participants in small groups responded to one another's developing course plans and assignments. Some of the small groups working together during the workshop were the interdisciplinary faculty teams who team taught CORE courses. They knew each other very well, watched each other's teaching on a regular basis, and knew that after the workshop they would actually teach the course they were planning and would continue to work closely together.

Walvoord's workshops emphasized linking writing assignments to course goals, using informal as well as formal writing, designing and sequencing assignments, stating criteria and expectations explicitly, getting lively interaction in class, and using draft response as well as other ways of guiding the writing process. WAC director Linda Hunt later collected faculty members' stories about how they had changed their teaching, and she published them in a 1992 in-house booklet. The stories focused on how faculty had related assignments more effectively to course goals, had given students fuller guidance, had instituted particularly successful assignments, or had introduced informal writing as a tool for learning.

Towson's program, much older than the others, had a more varied range of activities. In 1976, Towson's faculty revised its general education requirements to include a writing-intensive course, usually taken by students in their major field. By 1982, formal WAC faculty development was in place. Dowling coached faculty and observed classes. After 1984, two-day workshops presented an overview of the writing process, assignment planning, generating ideas, responding to drafts, and evaluating writing, with a segment on "writing-to-learn." These workshops were held in two adjacent, comfortable classrooms set up with tables that would seat four to six participants and include a coffee-and-donuts area. The presentations were structured, but the atmosphere was informal, with both leaders and participants exhibiting a great deal of enthusiasm. Analysis of the end-of-workshop participant responses from these workshops indicates a sense of pride among the participants that members of their own faculty could lead these workshops. Ninety-minute workshops concentrated on a single aspect of writing—using peer-response groups or helping students edit for style, for example. These Towson-led workshops were supplemented by a rich array of other resources in the area, including the Baltimore branch of the Maryland Writing Project, the Baltimore Area Consortium for Writing Across the Curriculum (a coalition of local colleges and K–12 schools), and neighboring universities and colleges (for more on the Baltimore Area Consortium, see Walvoord and Dowling 1990).

In addition, Towson's WAC coordinator, Fil Dowling, sponsored a Faculty Writers' Response Group for faculty (and has done so since 1985), which met regularly to respond to drafts written by its participants. Dowling, in the 1980s and early 1990s, also worked intensively one-on-one with twenty-one individual faculty, observing their WAC classes for three or four weeks, talking with their students, and consulting at length with faculty about their writing assignments, teaching modes, and evaluation methods.

Faculty Remembered WAC as a Community

Did the differences in the WAC events of each school create differences in our faculty members' memories and responses? We noticed some differences in emphasis when faculty described "What I learned was . . . ." Walvoord's workshop participants tended to reflect her emphasis on goal-driven course planning and articulation of teacher expectations. Fulwiler and Steffens's participants at UC reflected the emphasis on journals and collaborative student groups. Towson State participants reflected a wide diversity of the themes and emphases they had encountered. But those slight differences in themes were overshadowed by the shared sense among participants at all three schools that WAC events had given them a *community* which shared certain important characteristics. The communities of WAC often spoke to deeply felt needs. Faculty members' yearning for community was strong and consistent in our data. WAC experiences were not always perfect—and we will present in this chapter some accounts of disappointing or flawed communities as well as successful ones—but most faculty we interviewed felt very positive about their WAC experiences, and for many of the same reasons.

Characteristics of the

WAC community:

- *Safety*
- *Liberation*
- *Naming*
- *Support*
- *Validation*

Our findings here affirm those of the match-to-sample surveys we summarized in the introduction—that is, faculty reported enthusiasm and appreciation for the WAC workshops. But those surveys focused on the *teaching strategies* faculty had learned and, more generally, the *change or improvement* faculty judged WAC to have helped them realize. Our findings point to an additional factor—the *community* formed in WAC. Our data suggest that the experience of community was, for some faculty, as important, or more important, than particular teaching strategies.

What were faculty members' perceptions of the outstanding characteristics of WAC communities?

WAC Communities Were Safe and Liberating

One aspect of the WAC community which participants felt strongly about was its safety. The Faculty Writers' Response group at TSU, for example, was, as one faculty member put it, "a sanctuary away from invisible college politics—a safe place to expose one's thoughts and ideas."

Safety was the basis for liberation, a chance to explore, to risk, to be creative. A Whitworth musician remembers: "The liberal arts really means liberating things. And what this workshop did was to liberate me to be more creative in developing work that's meaningful to the students." A UC political scientist affirmed that, since the workshop, "I'm willing to risk more."

Part of liberation, too, was to be freed from fears. One fear some participants mentioned was that the workshop would require them to become English teachers. A Whitworth communications professor remembers:

> The greatest moment of relief for me came when Barbara [Walvoord] set me at ease by telling me I didn't have to become an English teacher to be involved in the workshop. I didn't have to be the final say on a student's grammar and punctuation. Going in, I had thought, "'Writing Across the Curriculum'—what I'm going to do is be transformed into adjunct faculty in English." I was relieved to find out I didn't have to be something that I wasn't prepared to be.

Another fear was connected to participants' own writing. In the TSU Faculty Writers' Response group, a health sciences faculty member recalled confessing to her writing group colleagues that she was neither motivated toward, nor successful in, writing for publication and asked for their advice: "Fil [Dowling] made the most startling suggestion—write about what you do best! I found this statement overwhelmingly forgiving." It was the key. She began to write about teaching and learning and to find publication outlets for her work. Her writing group became a safe place to overcome her writing fears.

WAC Communities Conferred the Power of Naming

Another aspect of community for faculty at all three schools was the workshops' function of naming—of giving language to participants' thoughts and experiences. A UC faculty member in criminal justice, who had been using writing in many ways, found the workshop helpful in "just knowing that there was this school of thought about using these different kinds of techniques." A communications faculty member at Whitworth muses about the power of naming both for teaching and learning:

> Something of what happened at the workshop for me is that the writing episodes in my teaching got renamed. Naming and renaming is extremely powerful. As teachers, we name and rename experiences with our students. As we name and rename with one another and for ourselves, our lives change.

Naming, an act performed in community, itself helped to build community.

WAC Communities Mutually Respected and Supported Their Members

Mutual support, respect, encouragement, and cordiality were other characteristics of the WAC community that many faculty appreciated. A UC professor recalls:

> Shakertown was an open discussion, and people weren't saying, "Oh, John did not write in complete sentences" or "His ideas don't seem to be consistent with what we're thinking." It was a supportive group, and I'm talking about the cordiality among people. They asked, "Did he really mean that?" instead of automatically assuming the comment was meant in a critical way. For example, I said, "We don't want to emasculate this thing. . . ." And some women colleagues were very offended by that term. . . . And I could understand it was an inappropriate term, but I didn't mean it in that way. . . . And they didn't immediately assume that I meant it in a very chauvinistic way. . . . We have to have a little bit of leniency and support or compassion for each other. That's what happens when the student writes something—you don't immediately say, "That's wrong." And that's what was so exciting to me about the workshop. You've got to establish an environment where the student is willing to say whatever he or she is thinking, and be encouraged to do that. Now, we can't get to that point if we, ourselves, can't get to that point. It was respect, mutual respect.

WAC Communities Validated the Importance of Teaching

For many faculty, another positive aspect of the WAC community was that it validated the importance of teaching. This was especially strong among faculty of those UC colleges that emphasized research (UC also includes some two-year and open-access colleges where teaching is the primary mission). Faculty felt that the workshop demonstrated some concern at the university level for the quality of teaching. One UC faculty member says:

> I just don't feel we talk very much about teaching in my department. I feel like I have a very different perspective on teaching than my colleagues do. I find that very frustrating.

Another UC faculty member adds:

We still live with an old reward system that says research and publication are really all that's important. If you can get a grant, what do you have to worry about this stuff for? Now, on the other hand, the provost was very supportive, and he funded these workshops.

The WAC communities, then, when they worked well for faculty, were characterized by safety, liberation, naming, support, and validation.

Divergent Voices

Two of our respondents pointed to elements that could spoil the sense of community: too much talking by leaders and a "true believer" mentality that quashed skepticism.

A TSU faculty member contrasts some of his workshop experiences with others:

Well, the [ninety-minute] faculty development workshops on the Towson campus are a mixed bag. Typically, you walk in, you sit down, people talk at you, and then you leave. But the series of seminars on teaching the adult learner, the [Johns] Hopkins [University] seminar on the syllabus as a planning tool, and the five or six other seminars that I took over the course of a couple of years—these were just excellent practical experiences where what was talked about was modeled at the same time.

One of our UC respondents resisted what he saw as the "true believer" mentality of the workshop:

I can remember having long discussions at the workshop with people we began to label as the "true believers." They insisted vehemently that all you have to do is be enthusiastic about this yourself and believe in it enough, and the students will do any exercise that you ask them to do. Classes that used to sit there sullen and silent will, all of a sudden, break forth into intelligent discussion. A lot of us just didn't buy it. . . . There was this wonderful scene at the workshop where we broke into little groups that were supposed to solve a particular problem about writing. The group I was in was supposed to solve the problem I just mentioned: What if the students won't play? What do you do? Well, it so happened that one of the most ardent of the true believers was in this group, and she spent the entire time insisting that there was no problem, that it would never happen that students wouldn't play, and that therefore we didn't need to come up with any answers. And I regret so much that it didn't occur to me to point out to her that she herself wasn't playing.

We believe this faculty member's experience points to the difficulties of the "resistance" or "conversion" frame we discussed in the introduction. This faculty member's report suggests to us that a "conversion" frame can also cause problems in the WAC communities themselves. Much more healthy, we believe, was the conclusion drawn about a UC workshop by another participant: "You don't have to be a convert."

Clearly, the same workshops can be perceived differently by different participants. These differences are influenced, no doubt, by many factors which the workshop leader does not entirely control—participants' personalities, moods, habitual ways of working, and understanding of community. But our findings suggest that the kind of community that WAC participants experience creates enduring memories and is crucial to WAC's impact upon faculty.

Faculty Saw the WAC Groups and Workshops as Models for Their Own Colleague and Classroom Communities

Many of our faculty saw their WAC experiences of community as a model for the kind of classroom communities they would like to create—classrooms where, in one professor's words, "you don't immediately say, 'that's wrong,'" and where "the student is willing to say whatever he or she is thinking about." That same theme comes through very strongly in a Towson State faculty member's story. As his Faculty Writers' Response Group responded to drafts of his textbook, he in turn developed ways of using student-response groups in his classes and then integrated that knowledge into his textbook and into his work with other teachers:

> The writing group—a peer-response group itself—demonstrated to me not only how to use the technique with my students, but also how to experience and appreciate the power of the process myself as a writer and teacher.

Many faculty created analogies in this way between their WAC communities and their own teaching. Fulwiler's (1981) sense that WAC workshops are more about "showing" than about "telling" seems borne out by our data from all the WAC experiences, even those whose content and emphasis were somewhat different than his. The demonstrated community of WAC becomes a model for participants' classrooms.

The ideal classroom community, as outlined by Parker Palmer (1983), closely resembles the WAC communities as we have described them. The "spaces for learning" we create in our classrooms, Palmer says, should have three characteristics: openness, boundaries, and an air of hospitality. An open environment removes impediments to learning around and within us, sets aside barriers behind which we hide, and helps us resist our tendency to clutter up our consciousness and our classrooms. Firm boundaries provide a structure for learning, a space that has edges, perimeters, and limits. A hospitable environment is one where we receive each other, a place for newborn ideas to emerge, where we lose our fear of not knowing. It would be possible to see the WAC workshops and groups, as faculty portrayed them, within Palmer's frame, though Palmer was describing classrooms, not faculty workshops. No wonder, then, that our faculty easily created analogies between their WAC communities and the classrooms they yearned to create. A later chapter will show that one of the most common reasons faculty gave for adopting or rejecting a particular WAC teaching strategy was whether or not that strategy helped them build the longed-for community in their classrooms.

Some Faculty Extended Their WAC Communities

We were struck, in our data, by powerful stories from those faculty members who had found ways of extending, across time and across disciplines or distances, the communities they formed in WAC. We include three of those stories here. Each represents a different site for community. Sociologist Don O'Meara, who teaches at one of the two-year colleges at UC, built community through his department's reworking of a course they all taught, through faculty development workshops on critical thinking, and through sessions of his national sociological society. Whitworth's Barbara Filo, in art, built community through working with a strong mentor and through team teaching. Towson's Barbara Kaplan Bass, in English, built community in a series of close-knit support groups, including an ongoing WAC Faculty Writers' Response Group and a women's studies group. All three stories also reflect the faculty members' increasing ability to bring their own students into community. These powerful stories suggest, we think, the importance of providing ways for communities to continue after WAC.

The first two stories are taken from interviews. The last, written by Barbara Bass herself and read for response in her TSU Faculty Writers' Response Group, is a more polished piece. The excerpts are fairly long, because we wanted to present enough scope to show the ways in which faculty extended community and to give our readers a sense of the rich and intricate connectedness of these faculty lives—a connectedness that we believe WAC and other faculty development programs need to understand and build upon.

Building Community through Department, Workshops, and Professional Conferences

—from a 1994 interview with Don O'Meara, Sociology, Raymond Walters, College of UC (two-year, open-admissions branch campus)

Community through departmental colleagues attending a workshop.

For the past four to five years, the other sociologists in the department and I had been looking at the intro sociology sequence because it didn't focus as much as we wanted it to on issues and problems. And we wanted to get more articulation with the main campus. A couple of the sociologists in the department and I had attended a couple of workshops on critical thinking. That probably stimulated our thinking about critical thinking even before the WAC conference. At first, I saw the WAC thing as a mechanism for the critical thinking. But then I began to see that WAC is critical thinking. And the WAC and the critical thinking became a stimulus. It seemed like, OK, this is the time to do it; the pieces are coming together.

Community through the national professional association.

Another piece was that I went to the American Sociological Association's national convention—I always try to get to that—and I discovered a new book on introducing critical thinking in the classroom.

So, the other sociologists in the department and I revised the third quarter of the intro sociology sequence. It now uses a lot of worksheets [Figure 5.1], students do lots of readings and articles, and then in class, there's a lot of group discussion on what these authors are saying and what they're not saying, what's good and bad about the articles, in terms of these principles of critical thinking developed in the book. It was astounding. In my classes, I went from students who didn't know the difference between a value and a fact, to the end when they would say, "Hey, that's a value, that's a fact. Hey, yeah, we know that." And they did. They really did. The course now does a good job in writing across the curriculum. It's very writing based, has lots of oral communication, and a good, sound structure on critical thinking.

**Guidelines for Completing
the 4-Step Critical Reasoning Worksheet**

Step 1: Identify the Five Topics of Reasoning

A. Definition of the Problem:
   1. Clearly *state* the basic thesis of the article.
   2. *List* any vague or undefined terms which are important to the thesis.

B. Cause-Effect Relationships:
   1. *List* the cause-effect statement(s) critical to the thesis.
   2. *List* any other relevant cause-effect statements.

C. Values:
   1. *Identify and list* any value terms which convey the author's basic value orientation.

D. Evidence:
   1. *List* the basic sources of evidence used in the author's argument.
   2. *Identify* each source of evidence as primary or secondary.
   3. Briefly *describe* the methodology used to collect primary evidence.

E. Solution (or Nonsolution):
   1. Briefly *describe* the author's solution to the problem.
   2. Briefly *identify* any nonsolutions which the author identifies.

Step 2: Criticize the Adequacy of the Five Topics

A. Definition of the problem:
   1. Is the thesis clearly stated?
   2. Are the key terms and concepts clear?
   3. Are the terms used consistently?

B. Cause-Effect Relationships:
   1. Are the causes complex or simple?
   2. Are the effects clearly linked to the causes?
   3. Are these links plausible?

C. Evidence:
   1. Are the sources of evidence identified?
   2. Are the data objective?
   3. Are the data accurate?
   4. Is the methodology clearly described?
   5. Are there drawbacks to the methodology?
   6. Are there any sweeping or hasty generalizations?
   7. Is the evidence communicated clearly?

Figure 5.1. Sample worksheet for Don O'Meara's sociology class.

Figure 5.1 continued

D. Values:
    1. Are the author's value criteria identified?
    2. Are there any values which you infer from the article?
    3. Are the values well defended by the author?
    4. Are the values distinguished from the evidence?

E. Solution:
    1. Is the solution stated clearly?
    2. Does the solution deal with the problem?
    3. Is the solution plausible?

Step 3: Summarize the Author's Line of Reasoning

    1. *Look over* your entries in Steps 1 and 2 and your narrative in Step 3.
    2. *Write a brief narrative* linking the five elements of the author's argument: thesis, principle cause-effect relationships, evidence, values, and solution.

Step 4: Criticize the Author's Line of Reasoning

    1. *Look over* your entries in Steps 1 and 2.
    2. *Write a brief narrative assessing* the author's argument.
        a. Is the argument coherent? If not, identify what is not coherent.
        b. Do the parts of the author's argument fit together logically? If not, identify the gaps.
        c. State briefly the principle strength and principle weakness of the author's argument.
        d. State brief overall personal assessment.

Community through departmental curriculum planning.

Those of us who taught it the first time will be meeting again to see what went well, what we want to revise, what we're going to do spring quarter. We're so happy with the way it went that we're probably going to revise Soc. 102, start integrating some of the critical thinking steps, so that, by the time they get to Soc. 103, they're even more prepared.

Challenges to community: integrating part-time faculty.

There are real challenges with doing that course because I have part-time people teaching it, too, and that's a real issue out here at this college. They have to be trained to teach the course, and there are even legal issues as to whether you can ask a part-time person to do that or not.

Barb [Walvoord] came out and spoke to my department on how to develop a general education course, and that was very helpful. [At UC, general education courses must have critical-thinking and communications components.] We had a little workshop with her. [It] overwhelmed my faculty [chuckles], but they had a real strong sense of what they had to do. So I think it was a very positive thing.

Community through departmental meeting with WAC leader.

Several of us have participated in the oral communication workshops. I haven't, but several others have. And we participated in another critical-thinking workshop.

Community through ongoing workshops.

Building Community through Team Teaching and Mentorship
—from a 1994 interview with Barbara Filo, Art, Whitworth

I think what I remember most about the workshop was the interaction of the other people. . . .

Community through mentorship.

I'd taken courses from Dr. Bill Youngs at Eastern. He teaches history, but he is very interested in writing. He writes himself, and then he requires quite a bit of writing from his students. I had three courses with him, and they were all writing intensive, and they drove me crazy, but were very valuable. And so I've used some of his ideas, and also his course certainly helped my own writing.

I've team taught . . . a number of courses [and on] the CORE team; also the "Introduction to Fine Arts" with Randy and Rick, and then later with Rick and Dick Evans. Sounds like a comedy team. And then I team taught with Corliss Slack. On the CORE team there was a change, so there were several people in that group. And then with the British Isles course I taught with Forrest and Arlin and Michael Bowen and Corliss again. And I can't remember about the others. Quite a number of different faculty members. And I've learned from all of them. It's just been wonderful to watch them teach. It lifts my spirits and makes me feel invigorated, and I want to get to my class and try this new thing.

Community through team teaching.

Building Community through Close-Knit Support Groups
"Tapped Resources"
—by Barbara Kaplan Bass, English, TSU

[Note: The following essay by Barbara Kaplan Bass, which she entitled "Tapped Resources," was written in response to our request that she write about what WAC had meant to her. Her Faculty Writers' Response Group at Towson State served as responders in the development of the essay.]

Students sprawl across the floor, oversized sheets of newsprint at odd angles underfoot, multicolored Magic Markers™ in hand. A faculty member passing by looks into the room and snorts, "What is this, third grade?"

Well, no, it's not third grade—it's—it's thirteenth grade. These are college freshmen, writing similes on newsprint to be displayed around the room: "Writing is like making orange juice—it's worth the effort, seeds and all!" "Writing is like having a tooth pulled—it's painful, but it has to be done." These composition students are comparing their writing experiences, making friends, creating a writing community.

While they are working I step out into the hall to track down my colleague. I locate him across the hall, behind his podium, lecturing to students who are obviously not participating in the making of meaning. He is probably repeating in his classes what his professors taught in theirs.

Who taught me? A third-grade language arts teacher from a rural county, a middle school teacher from the inner city, a women's studies instructor—too many to list here, but all have had a profound influence on who I am and how I teach. They released me from the lectern, from the tyranny of grading, and from the boredom of the five-paragraph theme. Most important, they connected me to an invaluable network of teachers from whom I continue to learn.

Before I opened myself to these connections, teaching for me, as for many others, had been a solitary profession. Good teachers knew all the answers and hoarded them in their private collections of lesson plans. During my college teaching practicum, my "cooperating" teacher told me that student teachers were "a necessary evil." I stumbled out into teaching, young, alone, and unsupported, and became a teacher's guide junkie, looking for quick classroom fixes, but not understanding why they worked or not.

When I was offered a visiting instructor's position at Towson State to teach [first-year] composition, I had no one to ask for advice. I went to a college bookstore and hunkered down amongst the handbooks and rhetorics piled on the shelves, looking for guidance, and—not knowing any better—chose one that mirrored the way I had been taught. I followed its prescriptions, but it didn't feel right. I was confused, but an admission of confusion would be an acknowledgment of incompetence. I stumbled on, not knowing there was a better way, teaching against my better instincts, remaining as alone in my college teaching as in my high school teaching.

Several years after beginning my college teaching, I was still using a traditional rhetoric, but supplementing it with articles on current issues, trying to create a course that was useful and practical, but still not articulating to myself my own teaching philosophy. When I was asked to participate in a workshop designed to mainstream women's studies into writing classes, I jumped at the opportunity to meet other faculty and to learn how other instructors taught composition. What I found there was my first real connection to a teaching network, a group of women committed to effecting change and establishing a community on campus. Our group unofficially expanded to include faculty from physical education, philosophy, and administrators from our university.

"What we do is *de*grading, not grading," I heard one of the women's studies members of our committee say. Yes, I thought, that's exactly how I feel. But I still wasn't brave enough to agree with her out loud.

"I am so frustrated with my advanced comp class. I'm not getting anywhere," another teacher complained. "I feel like my students resent my help."

I couldn't contain myself any longer: "You do, too? I thought I was the only one who felt that way!" We began sharing our teaching stories, drawing comfort from our mutual frustrations, discussing ways to improve our teaching.

Another women's studies faculty member offered: "All writing isn't argument. It doesn't have to be hierarchical. Have you ever seen a five-paragraph theme in real life?"

"It isn't? It doesn't? Well, no I haven't!" I responded. But what do I know, I thought to myself.

It turned out I knew quite a lot. During that year, the six of us learned from each other, experimented in our classrooms, traded theory as well as practice, and effected real change. We presented a panel at the annual [meeting of the] Conference on College Composition and Communication. I was able to abandon my old rhetoric text and handbook and approach the teaching of writing honestly for the first time. I could take some risks now. I was no longer alone.

At that point in my teaching career, I was still wedded to teaching the patterns of organization. Every rhetoric I had reviewed that summer in the bookstore had organized its chapters around those patterns. That format was even mandated by the English department, so I had assumed that it must be the way to organize my course. Before I chose my text for the next semester, I brought up this issue at one of our mainstreaming meetings. Those of us who taught this way felt uncomfortable with the method.

"How do you yourselves go about writing?" one of our group tossed out to us. We all agreed that we often did not know what we had to say until we began writing. We didn't always begin with the thesis statement that we insisted our students use. Often, one idea jumped backwards to connect with another, and another spiraled out to connect with nothing.

At our next meeting, another women's studies instructor brought us each a copy of *Women's Ways of Knowing* (Belenky et al. 1986). We discovered that most women write the way we do, recursively, not hierarchically. We decided that the next semester, we would teach the required patterns, but for two days rather than for fourteen weeks! I began *offering* the patterns to my students rather than forcing the patterns upon them, explaining that they may be used as a guide, not a strict prescription. Such a discovery was liberating. As a solitary teacher, I might never have given myself permission to abandon tradition and follow my instincts, to share my classroom practice with others and benefit from theirs.

The mainstreaming workshop also enabled me to do my own classroom research, opening up a part of me that is now crucial as I grow as a teacher. I had asked my students to write about an admirable character from a book of their choice. I was surprised to find that of my thirty-six students, both male and female, thirty-three had chosen male characters; the three who had chosen women had chosen the autobiographies of Joni Erikson and Jill Kinmont, women who were paralyzed—strong, yet immobilized women. The next semester I provided the students with books that had strong female characters—for example, *The Color Purple* and *The Stone Angel*—and gave this same assignment. This time thirty-five students chose women characters, and the one who didn't chose a compassionate male. My subsequent article based on this classroom research was accepted by the *Maryland English Journal*. I was now a published writer—an official researcher. Since then I have published regularly on pedagogical issues and have written a chapter for a book. With the help of my colleagues from across the curriculum, I found a voice.

The next semester, primed by my mainstreaming workshop experience, I had my eyes and ears open for more connections. One morning, as I hurried to class, a brochure lying on the corridor floor caught my eye. "Writing Matters," it said. "Well, yes it does," I thought. I was intrigued. A few weeks later I found myself at an extraordinary conference sponsored by the Maryland Writing Project, interacting with teachers from all disciplines and across all grade levels. What an opportunity to extend my network! I signed up for their five-week Summer Teacher Institute. In that dynamic workshop, it was the elementary participants who taught me about using newsprint and Magic Markers™, the middle school teachers who turned me on to webs and Venn diagrams. And in the years since that summer, I have been able to share with them, through MWP-sponsored study groups and conferences, the work I have been doing in raising student awareness about racism and sexism through writing, writing over time, and alleviating writing anxiety. The institute coordinators directed me to authors such as Donald Graves and Donald Murray, Linda Flower and Lucy Calkins, all writing and thinking about how students write, from first grade through college.

Perhaps the most valuable aspect of the Maryland Writing Project, though, is its focus on one's own personal writing—probably the scariest aspect of the summer for me. I didn't have time for personal writing. I had papers to grade, diapers to change, syllabi to organize, carpools to drive, and I certainly was not comfortable sharing my writing with anyone else, especially public school teachers. What could a third-grade teacher have to say about my writing that could be of any use?

That summer, though, for two afternoons a week, I met with three other institute participants in what would become my first official writing group. At our first meeting, too afraid to try a new piece, I brought an essay I had written years before and hoped it would pass muster. By the time of our second meeting, I felt comfortable enough to risk writing a piece about my adopted daughter, then ten years old, who had come to us with more than we bargained for. Another group member, a middle school English teacher from the city, wrote about her father who had passed away, whose voice she no longer could remember. Another, a high school social studies teacher from a rural county, wrote about becoming a grandmother at forty. The fourth member, a suburban elementary teacher, bared her soul about her teaching fears. By the end of that session, I couldn't wait to go home and write more. Since that time, I have continued to write personal essays, many of which have been published in local newspapers and magazines; the first essay that was accepted was the one I was brave enough to write for my MWP writing group.

By this time, I was hooked, primed for more faculty interaction, when I noticed in the *Towson State Faculty Newsletter* Fil Dowling's brief announcement for an interdisciplinary Faculty Writers' Response Group. I thought this new group might help guide me into more professional writing.

When I arrived at my first writing group meeting, I found several members of the English department, one from history, two from nursing, one each from health science, management, mass communications, and chemistry. The historian wrote poetry, the nurses were working on an article for a professional journal, one of the English faculty was preparing a presentation for a conference, and the mass comm professor was writing a chapter for a book. Not everyone brought something, but everyone shared ideas. Their drafts were messy, written on, some of the papers unfinished. After we had discussed the last piece, I hesitantly brought out the piece about my daughter that I had started during the Summer Teacher Institute. It was perhaps the tenth draft. My fears resurfaced: I was afraid they would judge me too harshly; I didn't know them well enough for them to see my writing, warts and all. As I sat there waiting for their comments, I realized that my students must feel this same fear when I ask them to share their writing with each other in class. Once I overcame my initial fear, this group gave me invaluable help. Our management member taught me about subheadings, our health science person helped me to organize, the mass communications person could see "the big picture," and everyone taught me new perspectives on words and language. Since then, I won't submit an essay to the newspaper, an article for publication in a journal, or a proposal for a conference without first running it by my group. We even developed a workshop for the Conference on College Composition and Communication where we demonstrated how valuable these faculty connections are and how a cross-disciplinary writing group can work.

The last two summers I have helped coordinate the Maryland Writing Project's Summer Teacher Institute. One of my favorite days during the workshop is when biologist Ginny Anderson comes by with her caterpillars or baby mice to share her ideas about writing in the sciences. As I look around the room at the new crop of participants who listen, fascinated by Ginny's ideas, I think about how far I've come, how much I've learned from teachers from every level and every discipline. Each summer I have seen experienced teachers on that same precarious perch I had been on—clinging to old ideas only because that is all they know, yet ready to fling them off. I also see brand new teachers who are beginning their careers as part of a supportive network, empowered from the start. At times, I envy them, saddened by how I shortchanged myself and my students for so long, relieved that I came to understand the power of connections, of writing, and of teachers themselves who have so much to offer. We are a too-frequently untapped resource:

> "Are you in room 109?" one of my colleagues asks. "What are those similes on the wall in there? Where can I get that paper they're written on? Does the department have Magic Markers™?"
>
> Another stops me in the hall. "I've seen your students working together in groups on their writing. Can you explain to me how you organize them?"
>
> Any time.

6 How Did WAC Affect Philosophies and Attitudes about Teaching?

The workshop made a difference in how I think.
—Biology, Whitworth

In the previous chapter, we reported that faculty saw themselves immersed in a river of change that constantly took them into new teaching ventures. They'd been changing before they came to WAC, and they expected to change after WAC. We noted, too, that a number of faculty credited WAC with enhancing the pace or direction of change ("The workshop encourages you to experiment") and with encouraging them to be self-directors of their own change ("You don't have to be a convert"). This chapter and the next explore in more detail how WAC influenced the changes that faculty made *in their teaching.*

In the introduction, we discussed the problems inherent in establishing the "influence" of WAC (or anything else) on faculty behavior (page 26, this volume). To help us address the question of the influence of WAC on teaching, we have relied primarily on two data sources. One is faculty reports. We reasoned that faculty members themselves often know whether a particular idea or practice was influenced by WAC. They may overstate that influence, however, in the interview situation through a desire to please the WAC researchers or because WAC has been unnaturally highlighted from a mosaic of otherwise intermingled threads and influences. Also, some deeper reasons for their adoption of a particular practice—reasons rooted in psychological or sociological factors, in family, culture, class, or gender—may be largely invisible to the faculty member and are beyond the reach of this study. Nonetheless, many faculty were very clear and concrete in describing how WAC had influenced their teaching strategies.

A second type of data from which we trace the influences of WAC are the syllabi and other course documents, the classroom observations, and our own participant-observer knowledge of what happened in most of the WAC workshops and groups. Being present in all these places helped us to recognize when a workshop idea appeared later in a faculty syllabus or teaching practice.

On the basis of that data, then, we address in this chapter the ways in which WAC appears to have influenced faculty members' teaching philosophies and attitudes and (in the next chapter) their classroom strategies. Since our data are not consistent in type, we did not code the responses, and we do not here present percentages of faculty who were influenced in various ways. Rather, our data allowed us to read and reread, looking for themes that appeared in various guises and in various types of data.

Our first conclusion from the data is that the depth, amount, and type of influence varied, but *some sort* of influence was reported by nearly all the participants. In the 1991 survey of 117 UC Population A faculty (page 36, this volume), 99 percent said they had changed their teaching in some way as a result of the workshop. Kalmbach and Gorman (1986) found that 82 percent of their ninety Michigan Technological University faculty said their teaching had improved as a result of a workshop. Other research we summarized in Chapter 1 also supports this conclusion that WAC results in change. But what kinds of change?

Faculty reported that *individual WAC teaching strategies* might be altered, passed over, or rejected for certain reasons. But many faculty viewed the changes in their *theories, habits of mind, confidence, enthusiasm, and relation to students* as contributions they would not later reject or lose, but would further build upon. They tended to frame their statements about these contributions with markers such as "The most useful thing for me" or "What I most vividly remember." The most long-lasting outcomes of WAC workshops for faculty may not be in individual teaching strategies, such as previous research has often measured as WAC outcomes, but in changes in teaching philosophies and attitudes.

Our evidence suggests five ways in which the WAC experiences influenced faculty members' teaching philosophies and attitudes:

- *theories* about the nature of teaching and learning;
- *habits of mind* during the planning and teaching process;
- *sense of confidence* in teaching;
- *enthusiasm* for teaching;
- *roles in relation to students.*

Faculty Developed Their Theories about Teaching and Learning

Faculty often reported that their WAC experiences had led them to new insights about the nature of writing, teaching, and learning, insights they often expressed as declarative statements with "writing" or "students" or "learning" or "teachers" as the subject. The theories faculty reported to us often concerned:

- coming to see learning as an active collaboration between student and teacher;
- seeing new possibilities for their role as teachers and for the role of writing in the classroom.

Sometimes faculty reported having been working toward such theories prior to the workshop, but some reported making a sharp turn in their ideas about teaching and learning. Below we present a sample of the theories faculty expressed to us.

"There Are Different Ways of Asking Students to Communicate"
—Math, UC

[Note: This faculty member mentions that a number of math faculty had been to the two-day Shakertown workshop, and others to a 2-1/2-hour on-campus workshop just for math faculty. As a result, he says,]

I think that the basic idea that there are different ways of asking students to communicate other than computation tests has disseminated throughout the department quite a lot, and I suspect it's almost to the point where people don't even give it a lot of thought now. It's sunk in. WAC was certainly what got us thinking about educational ideas.

"Writing Has Stages"
—History, Raymond Walters College of UC

The workshop gave me the idea of thinking more of writing as having stages. And if all you do is get the writing at the end, then it's too late to do anything other than grade it.

"Students Need to Internalize"
—Architecture, UC

Students need to internalize material in order to understand it, and the process of writing or other processes of personal expression are very critical in that process. That to me was the real critical issue of the workshop, and that's been very effective.

"I Shifted My Philosophy of How People Learn —from More Passive to More Interactive"
—Adjunct Political Science, College of Evening and Continuing Studies, UC

Allowing students to step back from what's being discussed or read, and to concoct their own version of it, has become much more important in my class. I had been through some interpersonal and reflective kinds of training, and I would include the Shakertown workshop as part of that. I think there were enough of those kinds of sessions that I really had shifted my philosophy about how people learn—from more passive to more interactive.

"You Have to Start Where the Students Are"
—Math, University College, UC (two-year, open-admissions)

I had been going this direction, but in my own little narrow way. The workshop helped keep my interest up, lit some fires underneath, and gave me materials to work with. . . . You have to start where the students are. You've got to get down with them, get into the dirt.

"Give as Much Guidance as Possible"
—Music, Whitworth

The most important thing I remember was how important it was to give students a lot of detail, a lot of instructions. Sometimes we think that we should just tell students and they should know what they're supposed to do. I had heard in my doctorate, too, to give detail and help guide students. And the other things were to respond to drafts, do conferencing, and things like that. Professor Walvoord's approach was to give as much guidance as possible.

"Teaching Writing Goes on Over and Over throughout a Student's Career"
—History and Political Science, Whitworth

What I most vividly remember—and this is a transition I made—at that time I thought teaching writing was something that only people in English did. And they ought to be able, with a good, solid [first-year] composition course, to bring students up to speed. So then I could just read papers that were written at an acceptable college level. And I think I realized in the workshop that teaching writing is something that goes on over and over and over throughout a student's career.

Faculty Developed New Habits of Mind

Faculty often reported having developed new habits of mind—that is, ways of thinking during the planning and teaching process. Their reports on this score support Sipple's (1987) study of think-aloud tapes made as WAC faculty planned writing assignments. She found that WAC faculty planned courses differently from faculty who had not been through a workshop. WAC faculty were more oriented toward learning goals and more likely to use assignments for learning, not just for testing knowledge.

The selections below, taken from 1993–1995 interviews and supported by our other data, indicate some of the new habits of mind that faculty reported.

"It Caused Me to Think through My Goals for Each Course"
—Religion, Whitworth

I think the most useful thing for me was the discussion of the relationship between goals (learning objectives) and curriculum and the way that writing can serve those ends. And that caused me to go back and think through more carefully what the exact goals are for each one of my courses and how writing assignments might serve those goals. I found that very useful.

"The Workshop Made Me Worry More about Assignments"
—Biology, Whitworth

The workshop made a difference in how I think about assignments. It made me worry more about assignments. I look at them and I think, "Well, crud, I mean, what would I expect a student to actually *do* with this? What do I really think I'm going to see at the end of this process?" And I've concluded that if I don't have a good picture of that in my mind, then either it's not a well-written assignment, or I'm not ready to give the assignment. A couple of times on the CORE team, I think it has made me a bit of a nuisance, if we're under the gun to get this paper topic ready.

Faculty Gained Confidence in Their Teaching

A common theme was that faculty had gained a new sense of confidence. This sense of confidence came partly from the naming and legitimizing that we mentioned in the chapter on what WAC experiences meant to faculty. It also came from a sense of collegial support, of community.

"I Understood It Well Enough to Have Confidence"
—International Business, TSU

What really helped my confidence was not somebody in the workshop talking at me, but someone saying something, and then I was able to walk through and see, in fact, how it happened, and I could feel how the happening felt. Then I understood it well enough to have the confidence to try it myself. Prior to that time I [didn't have] the confidence because I didn't have the understanding.

"With Growing Confidence, I Began to Use the Process with My Students"
—Speech and Mass Communications, TSU

I shall never forget what the writing group gave me at a crucial time in my career—the pleasure of acceptance and the stimulation of listening and learning among peers. With growing confidence, I began to use the process more and more with my students.

Faculty Gained a Renewed Enthusiasm for Teaching

"The Workshop Just Turned Me On"
—Music, Whitworth

The other thing I like about those kinds of workshops is the intellectual stimulation. The WAC workshop just turned me on to these ideas.

"It Cements Your Commitment to Teaching"
—Adjunct Political Science, College of Evening and Continuing Studies, UC

I think one of the more valuable things about the workshop was the experience of thinking about the quality of your teaching as felt by students, as experienced by them. It forces you to go back to your philosophies. Lots of mundane things shove aside these big, deep thoughts, and it helps to have support and to be in an atmosphere where people are discussing this, [where] people are assuming we want quality teaching. It helps you to recommit your energy to that. It cements the commitment.

Faculty Changed Their Roles in Relation to Students

The following story illustrates the final point we're making in this chapter—that for some faculty, WAC resulted in a change in their relations to students. But it also illustrates all the other points. It's the story of a teacher's long-term struggle to become more human toward his students. The struggle is played out in many ways: through assignments; through the syllabus and handouts; through what the teacher did in the classroom; through how he handled himself in face-to-face conversations with students; and through how he thought of himself and his students. It was a shift in philosophy and attitude influenced not only by the WAC seminar, but by other factors as well—graduate school experiences, words of advice from colleagues, a National Endowment for the Humanities summer seminar, and a Fulbright Fellowship in Korea.

"There's More of a Sense of 'Let's Work Together'"
—Arlin Migliazzo, History, Whitworth

The WAC seminar made me rethink the tone of my syllabus.

I realized that in plugging all the holes, I didn't leave a whole lot of room for the students.

The syllabus was devoid of much humanness.

I don't use the freewrite to gauge how well they're writing. It's more to get them to hook into concepts.

Faculty: The WAC seminar made me rethink the tone of my syllabus. When I was a student, I didn't learn as much as I could have because I knew what the shortcuts were, and the teachers left them there. You could drive a truck through the gaps—and I did. So, as a teacher, what I did for years, and it's still a temptation, is to try to plug the holes so students have no recourse but to learn. But by the time I came to the seminar, I had been thinking, "Does this sound like me? Do I like it?" And I realized that in plugging all the holes, I didn't leave a whole lot of room for the students.

The other thing was the way the syllabus came off. I hate to use the word "authoritarian," but it just came off like, "We do this; we do this; we do this." It was devoid of much humanness, I suppose. I had an attendance policy I didn't like—that was part of it. Finally, I said, "This is nuts. I shouldn't do this." So I rewrote practically the whole syllabus. And a lot of my handouts now are done in a different vein. There is more of a sense of "Let's work together on this; these are ways I think you can learn best."

Interviewer: Besides the syllabus change, have you initiated any other of the changes talked about in the workshop?

Faculty: What I've moved to a lot is the freewrite. I remember saying, "If a student writes and you never grade it, doesn't that kind of leave them hanging?" And you [Linda Hunt] and Barbara [Walvoord] said, "That's not the function of the assignment." So, when the thought hits me or when I think we need to shake things up a little bit, I'll just ask them to take out a piece of paper: "For the next five minutes, I'd like you to write a letter to Joseph Stalin and tell him, 'This is how you should fix the union.'" And then I'll look at some of the papers. I don't use it as a gauge to determine how well they're writing or anything like that. It's more to get them to hook into concepts.

Interviewer: The other thing I remember talking about at the seminar is that because you are big [both laugh] and you have a forceful voice, the authority issue is sort of automatic by your presence.

Faculty: Yeah. I had a student today who was asking a question. So I walked over and sat down across the table from her, since I'm pretty tall. I try to do that for male students, too, but I'm particularly aware of it for female students because of the size differential.

Another thing I've done is dress more informally. I remember I had a colleague when I first started teaching, and he said that a suit and tie communicate certain things. And he was a suit-and-tie kind of guy. Well, I can be, but I don't necessarily like to be.

.   .   .   .

The biggest change in terms of structure is how I do major research assignments. It was really intriguing to me, the approaches that we experimented with in the WAC seminar. So what I do—and I can show you the syllabus— is, about the fourth week, we talk about how to develop a major research paper. And I have four steps and four handouts. The first handout talks about the thesis argument: what it is, why you have it, what it does. I use my own work, pieces that have been successful and that have not been successful, to illustrate.

And then about three weeks later, I give them the second handout, on the plotting web. I really like that. I talk about how I wrote my dissertation and how so often we're taught that we've got to put every dumb little thing on the outline. And I said—again reflecting my own struggle with balancing creativity and analysis— "Outlining can stifle your creativity." I think the plotting web lends itself more to creativity and spontaneity and better organization. And then I have a sample of one I made up about Theodore Roosevelt. It shows my thesis and the plotting lines. So then I say, "I would like you, on such and such a day, to submit a honed thesis, and then from that thesis, the thesis argument and the plotting web. And I'd like four more sources." And I always have to work with the students because half of them still don't seem to get that you're *arguing* something.

Then a few weeks later I give them the third handout— a speed draft [Figure 6.1]. It comes, again, directly from my own experience with both the old take-it-off-the-note card-and-outline method and my experience in graduate school. I remember when I first started graduate school, one of the recent Ph.D.s said, "The way you write a chapter is you look at your notes and then put them away and write." And I looked at him with horror, and I thought, "How can you possibly do that?" Well, I did the first chapter that

The biggest change in terms of structure is how I do major research assignments.

I looked at him with horror and thought, 'How can you possibly do that?'

HI 488W   **Research Project**   **Arlin Migliazzo**
                                         Step Three

The Speed Draft

Before proceeding to this stage of your project, the vast majority of the research must be completed. This does not mean that other sources should not be explored (especially if you are waiting for interlibrary loan materials). But it does mean that enough of the note taking and bibliographic work has been done so that you can clearly define and flesh out the sections of your paper as represented in your plotting web. Do not be overly concerned if the plotting web that you initially presented to me needs some revision as you get deeper into the research. That is as it should be. *Remember, even at this stage, you are working with tentative interpretations.* It is natural to expect that your thinking and your organizational schema for the project are still in something of a state of flux. Once you are at the point where most of the available sources have been mined, you are ready to write your speed draft. The speed draft is essentially a rough draft of the paper with a rather significant twist. It must be written at one sitting without referring to outlines, notes, books, or a plotting web. Before you are ready to rise in revolt, let me explain the rationale for this type of drafting process.

When you tie yourself to a plotting web, outline, or note cards, there are at least three major hindrances which block your creativity and inhibit the development of that "artsy" side of history we have been talking about. First, since you have done all this work, there is a powerful tendency to cram *everything* into the draft. As a result, you are so concerned about finding a place for all your research, that this concern overrides completely the narrative style you use to communicate your research. And we have already noted that it does not matter how wonderful your research is if you cannot communicate it to others in an engaging manner. Second, constant referral to a plotting web places an inordinate amount of emphasis on putting all your research in the right place. Strict adherence to the web *while writing the draft* will kill creativity just as surely as will constant checking of note cards. Finally, relying on notes, webs, and so forth while writing the draft will almost surely pull you off your main thesis argument. You may have found a place for all your research and put all your research nuggets in just the right places, but dollars to doughnuts, you will have failed to build a logically convincing or very readable draft. Therefore, to write the speed draft, follow these brief instructions:

1. Decide which day you will write the draft, and then count three to five days prior to that date.

2. Find a time during each of those days when you can methodically review your plotting web and each of your note cards.

3. On the day you have decided to write the draft, *put away all your note cards and sit down with a pen and paper.* Begin writing, filling in the organization and details you recall from your research. *Do not worry about citations.*

4. Continue writing until you have exhausted your store of knowledge. Put down your pen, put your name on the back of the draft, and do not look at it again until you turn it in to me at the beginning of class.

Figure 6.1. Speed draft assignment.

way, and that was it. I've never *not* done it that way. So I tell the students that story.

So once I get the speed drafts, I have a week to look at them, and then I dismiss class for a week and conference with each student for twenty to twenty-five minutes. I don't do anything with grammar. I look at how it fits together organizationally. I really try to emphasize the clear thesis statement. And does all the information that the student provided support the thesis argument in some way? Is there extraneous stuff here where maybe the creative juices got flowing a little too much and we're off into something else? And maybe it would be better not to put that in this paper. That's for the student's next project.

I dismiss class for a week and conference with students.

Interviewer: How would you describe the payoff in that?

Faculty: The average grade has gone up, but not as much as I'd hoped. I would like to see everybody in that 3.7 to 4.0 category, and I don't see them there. So I'm still working on that. But I've probably taught writing-designated classes about seven times now since the seminar, and I don't think I've had anyone earn below a "C."

The average grade has gone up, but not as much as I had hoped. I'm still struggling.

The issue I'm still trying to work with is—what if a student is late turning in the thesis and the four sources or the plotting web? It really kind of gums things up. So I still struggle with that.

The thing that was really helpful about the WAC seminar was just crafting assignments that hopefully would help people think and write better. But it also helped me focus more on what kind of presence I really want to project in class. That's a pedagogical issue that we don't really talk about, but I think it's extremely important. I realized that *my* perception of me was very different in some cases from the *students'* perception of me. I think the way to become a better teacher is to have those things line up. I need to see myself the way students see me. Or vice versa.

The seminar helped me to focus on the kind of presence I really want to project in class.

Even the way the plotting web project, the thesis argument handout, and all those things are put together is very different from the way I put things together five or six years ago. I think that it projects a different sense of what I'm here for. And I think that's been demonstrated on my student evaluations. I think I have seen a better sense of connectedness to the students. Obviously, there are some issues that still have to be worked on, but I think that the WAC workshop gave me the opportunity to work on not just the assignment I give to students, but *how* I give them

My handouts project a different sense of what I'm there for.

the assignments, how I portray what I think needs to happen in class. That's real helpful.

Interviewer: Have there been things from the seminar that have not worked?

It put me in the position of being the punisher. So I trashed that puppy.

Faculty: Before the seminar, I was going through and correcting all my students' grammatical mistakes. And Barbara [Walvoord] said, "Don't do that. That's not gonna help 'em; *they* have to find it." So I went to a system where I just put a check next to the line. And she talked about not even accepting a paper if it had too many check marks, but just handing it back for revision. So I wrote right on the syllabus if there are five errors on any one page, I'll turn it back and not read it. And it was *disastrous!* I think in the first set of forty papers, maybe six of them got through. It was horrible for me as well as for the students. They felt like they couldn't do anything right. And the papers just kept coming back and coming back, and I thought, "This is terrible! I can't ever get on top of this." And it put me in the position of being a punisher. So I trashed *that* puppy!

I also trashed revision. They've got to decide what they're going to do. Give them ownership.

And I also trashed revision. I tried it in a survey class. I still give them the option of giving me the rough draft ahead of time. But I don't say, "Okay, turn this paper in, and then you can revise it if you want to." In a survey class, where they have two or three short papers, after the first one comes back, I say, "If I can help you think through how to do the next one better, why don't you come in?" And in a class of forty, I usually get between five and eleven or twelve people. You see, it gives them ownership. They've got to decide what they're going to do. Let *them* decide from the get-go. Whereas, just after I took the WAC seminar, with the revision option after the papers were handed in, it was "Well, I'll see if you measure up, and then you can decide whether you're going to turn the paper back in." I can't do that. It's too much.

Interviewer: Can you describe peak moments in your teaching career?

Faculty: There were two. One happened probably six or seven years ago. We had a student here who was really hard to get along with, a nontraditional student. And I felt like I went the extra mile for this person and tried to work things out, but I'd been pushed to the limit by her. In my "Pacific Northwest History" class, she said something, and I just snapped. I still remember where she was sitting. I didn't yell or scream, but I put her in her place. And I realized as soon as I did that what I'd done. It's one of those things that after you say it, there's no way you can get it back. The whole tenor of the class changed. Oooooh! I couldn't get myself back on track. The students were obviously just as surprised, because I don't think anyone had ever heard me do that before. It was just horrible. I got out of class and thought, "What am I going to do?" Then I said, "Well, it's her fault. She did it." But by the end of the day, I knew what I had to do. I had to apologize to the whole class. Especially to her. So I made a time to see her before I saw the whole class, and I said, "I want to apologize for doing that. I would like to apologize in front of the class, because I think the class was part of that, and I want the students to know that we have worked toward reconciliation." She said, "That'd be fine."

I knew what I had to do. I had to apologize to the whole class.

So the next day I went into class and I said, "I want you to know that I was out of line. I'm not the perfect person. You saw that very much the other day." And I said a couple of other things about reconciliation and forgiveness. Then I said, "Okay, let's go on." And what was so neat after that is I got at least one note from a student, and I think other students talked to me. They'd never seen any prof do that before. And that has nothing to do with content. It has everything to do with presence.

That has nothing to do with content. It has every-thing to do with presence.

And the other peak moment does, too. Usually, when I talk about the sixties in the survey class, I give a lecture on Vietnam, and I play some rock music of the time. And this time I thought, "I'm not going to do that." I'm getting away from trying to stay to my notes. So I decided to go in and just tell them what it was like to be sixteen in 1968, and Martin Luther King Jr. gets killed, and then Robert Kennedy gets killed. I always struggle with how much to tell stories. Is it condescending? Is it trying to make too much out of my own experience? But this time I thought, "I don't care. I'm just going to see how this works." So I went in and pulled my draft card out of my wallet and told them about my visit to the draft board. Then I started to talk about Martin Luther King Jr. and Robert Kennedy and what it was like to live in L.A. and have that happen. And I told them, "I'm never going to take this draft card out of my wallet. I'm going to die with this in my wallet." And I started to crack up. I mean, I couldn't hold my composure. I couldn't go on. I didn't have any notes. I had my draft card and my memories, and that was it.

It had every-
thing to do
with connec-
tion, with
people and
humanness.

I think I scared some students. But also I had students come up and just say, "Man, that was—I never heard that before." It wasn't *content* at all. I think it was more how much I am willing to risk in front of the students. And that was a little *too* scary, that one. I was really out of control for a few seconds. But maybe, in a sense, that was good because they saw how close that really was. I mean, even though it was twenty-five years ago, it's just right there for me. And it had little to do with content and everything to do with connections, I think—with people and humanness.

We were struck by the importance that our faculty respondents attributed to their changes in philosophies, habits of mind, enthusiasm, commitment, and relation to students. The match-to-sample data we summarized in the introduction, and the "resistance" case studies with their emphasis on "my ideas" being adopted or resisted, perhaps have missed the most important outcomes of WAC. Individual teaching strategies may shift and change after WAC, as the story above and the accounts in the next chapter show. But WAC's most important outcome may be that underneath the shifting strategies, underneath the teacher's necessary accommodation to real-life constraints, lies a deeper stratum of faculty life—a stratum of belief, attitude, habit, commitment, and community—that can be changed, in some cases profoundly.

7 WAC Teaching Strategies: What Worked, What Didn't, and Why

What works, that's the main thing.
—Sociology, UC

In the previous chapter, we discussed the data on which we based our conclusions about the influences of WAC on teaching. That chapter dealt with the theories, habits of mind, confidence, enthusiasm, and new roles that WAC fostered. The same data sources (and the same problems with demonstrating WAC's "influence") inform this chapter about specific teaching strategies. But in addition to those faculty self-reports, syllabi, and other documents, here we also examine the survey data, particularly from UC and from Whitworth, which asked faculty what WAC strategies they were using.

Defining a WAC Strategy

To assess whether faculty have used WAC strategies or changed their strategies as a result of WAC, we must first define both "strategy" and "WAC." We define a teaching strategy as a deliberate action of the teacher, intended to result in student learning. Typical "WAC" strategies that were frequently named in the previous research and were used in the workshops on our three campuses include various kinds of informal writing ("journals," "prewriting," "informal writing," "ungraded writing"), explicit instructions and guidance for assignments, peer collaboration, teacher and peer feedback on drafts, and others.

Faculty in our study were frequently explicit, concrete, and confident about crediting specific strategies to WAC. Often, their definitions of a WAC strategy seemed consonant with what our records and memories indicated had been presented in the WAC program. For example, a UC criminal justice faculty member told us that the WAC workshop had led her to use informal writing in new ways to deal with racial tensions in her class.

However, some faculty had definitions of WAC strategies that were different from ours. A few confidently declared that they weren't using journals or peer collaboration; however, their classroom documents or their own statements later in the interview showed that they had, in fact, been using those strategies by *our* definition. Sometimes faculty were not sure whether something they were doing in the classroom would be classified as WAC. For example, a UC mathematician described how her department is instituting "laboratory sheets" in which students would be "asked to do various things and explain what they have done and what their conclusions are and why—not just give a numerical answer." Then she added, "I'm not sure if that's exactly what 'Writing Across the Curriculum' means." And later, she remarked, "All this is very different from students keeping journals and expressing themselves." She had not found "journals" useful in math classes, she explained, and counted herself as not having used them. So how should she be scored—as having used journals because we think so, or not using them because she thinks so?

> *"In using prewriting, I have students make lots of lists to stimulate discussion. So I don't know if that counts to you, when you're talking about writing."*
>
> —Political Science, UC

Faculty, as we have said (page 63, this volume), talked about the usefulness of the "naming" that went on in WAC. However, faculty members' WAC terms were not always consistent. In the face of this confusion, then, we tried to listen to faculty, to hear what *they* thought WAC was, what impact they thought WAC activities had had on their classroom strategies, and how those strategies had grown and changed.

In the end, we believe, the more relevant question is not whether faculty have adopted WAC strategies as *we* would define them, but what happened, as a result of WAC, to *their* strategies—for no classroom is without strategies, and the introduction of WAC is not the dropping of pebbles into an empty jar, but an influence upon what are, and must remain, *the faculty members'* strategies, born in their own situations, incorporated into their own teaching philosophies, twisted by their constraints of time and resources, and wonderfully transformed by their enthusiasm and creativity.

And though they were willing, for our benefit, to try to trace the origins of their strategies, faculty seemed not to have lost any sleep over whether or not a strategy was WAC. Sometimes they honestly could not remember where a strategy or an idea had come from or trace WAC influences upon it. What stood out to faculty were strategies that either "worked" or did not.

Strategies That "Worked"; Strategies That Were Used

We believe that the notions of "adopting" and "resisting," from the literature we reviewed in the introduction, need to be reexamined from the faculty members' points of view. Faculty do not see themselves as resisters, but as sensible people trying to find what "works."

Our data suggest that faculty will go to considerable lengths to use a teaching strategy they think is "working." They will try to retain it even if their classes get larger, other constraints interfere, or the strategy entails more work. Thus the key issue, we think, is not whether a faculty member is using a particular strategy that researchers name or whether a faculty member is "resisting" WAC strategies, but how faculty members decide whether a strategy works, and hence, whether to use it or not.

Faculty Used Similar Criteria for Judging a WAC Strategy to Have Worked or Not Worked

An important finding of this study is that faculty used the same criteria for saying that a WAC strategy had "worked" as for saying that it had "not worked," for adopting WAC strategies as for rejecting them. Faculty criteria focus on whether the WAC strategies did four things:

- *Community:* Did the strategy help build engagement and community in the classroom?
- *Learning:* Did the strategy lead to enhanced student learning?
- *Feasibility:* Was the strategy consonant with teachers' time pressures and other constraints?
- *Fit:* Did the strategy fit teachers' philosophies, priorities, and styles of teaching?

It was the application of these criteria, rather than "resistance" to WAC per se, that influenced faculty to use or not use WAC strategies.

Faculty with different teaching styles and personalities tried WAC strategies with different types of students, different class structures, different disciplines—and all of these factors seemed to influence whether the WAC strategies "worked." We even found that the same faculty member tried the same strategy in two different situations, discovering that it worked well in one situation but poorly in the other.

Faculty did not report themselves as particularly surprised by this variety. They saw themselves as constantly trying to find the proper *fit* between the situation and their own teaching strategies. They did not see themselves as converts or resisters to WAC, but as self-directed, rational human beings, trying to be better teachers in varied and complex circumstances, and using sensible criteria to determine whether a particular teaching strategy was working well in a particular situation.

Most Faculty Found Some WAC Strategies That Worked and Some That Did Not

In any single faculty member's story, strategies adopted and strategies abandoned were often inextricably combined. And decisions about strategies were inextricably part of the teacher's ongoing goals, theories, experiences, types of students, constraints of time and teaching load, and so on. Strategies are not successful or unsuccessful in a vacuum; nor is any strategy successful or unsuccessful for all teachers. Rather, a strategy is successful or not in a particular context and in the hands of a particular professor who uses it within the framework of his or her own goals, situations, reasons, and contexts. A WAC program, then, is not so much presenting a gospel as presenting a smorgasbord.

The following faculty stories illustrate how faculty evaluated whether a strategy "worked." They illustrate the complexity of the world to which faculty must bring specific teaching strategies discussed or modeled in WAC.

The first four stories present strategies that clearly and resoundingly "worked" for the faculty member and were retained during a period of at least several years. (For other descriptions of strategies that worked, see pages 69, 84, 85, 105, 108, 111, 113, and 133, this volume.) The later stories present more complex mixtures of strategies that either worked or did not work.

Strategies That Worked, #1
—Richard Evans, Music, Whitworth

[Note: During his 1990 faculty workshop, Evans developed an assignment that he was still using when we interviewed him in 1994. Printed below are excerpts from his 1992 description in Hunt's booklet and from his 1994 interview. Figure 7.1 is his assignment sheet. Based on research findings that people who dislike a certain piece of music may come to like it after multiple listenings, the assignment asks students to listen to a piece of modern music six times, writing about it in different ways throughout the listenings. The assignment "works" for Evans because it results in student learning—specifically, students come to appreciate modern music in new ways. It leads to community as students get involved, express their appreciation, and give Evans the highest student evaluations ever. It also enhances Evans's role within his own professional community, as colleagues appreciate and use his assignment.]

[From the 1992 Hunt booklet:] "Introduction to Music Literature" is the first course in which music majors encounter writing about music. Such writing is expected to be much more intentional than writing about music in a nonmusic course. During the first year of teaching the course, Spring 1990, I assigned students the task of writing three to five pages about a composer, a composition, or a form/genre. The papers were interesting but rather routine.

Before, I had just said, "Write about this composer and this composition."

I attended the first-year workshop in May 1990. As the workshop progressed, a piece of significant research in music learning theory began to merge with an idea for a writing assignment with much more learning significance. Students are sometimes reluctant to accept the music of our time. During the workshop I developed a plan for meeting this challenge. Research indicates that students tend to prefer those pieces they listen to at least six times. If this is so, I thought, maybe a writing assignment that included repeated listening would improve student attitudes toward modern music.

During the workshop, I developed a plan.

The new writing assignment asks students to select one of eight compositions from the twentieth century. Using a guide sheet I give them, they listen to the piece six times during the term. They research the piece, its composer, its style, its form, etc. After the first listening and the research, they submit a rough draft of the background researched material and their reaction to the first listening. That serves as the first two sections of the final paper. The third section of the final paper is the student's reaction after listening to the composition for the sixth time.

Students had to listen to a piece six times and write about it over time.

Let student comments from the final part of the assignment speak for its success:

Assignment Sheet

Purpose:

The purpose of this paper is to provide an in-depth acquaintance with a significant musical composition of the twentieth century. This assignment will combine background knowledge with your reflections upon listening, to increase your understanding of twentieth-century music.

Procedures:

You are to listen six times to one of the compositions listed below. Numbers at the end of the title rate the difficulty of listening and comprehension. These works are on reserve in the music office.

[Compositions such as Bartok's *Miraculous Mandarin* and Stravinsky's *Rite of Spring* are listed.]

After listening to the piece for the first time, you are to write the second third of the paper, answering the following question:

Thesis: This piece is (important) (not important) to me for the following reasons:

You should also answer the following questions:

1. What was the date of your first listening?
2. What was most striking in this piece?
3. Did you find anything in the piece you would like to listen to again? What was it?
4. Do you think you might learn to like this piece?
5. What in this piece sounds like something else you have heard? What is it?

After you have written the above, you are to research matters surrounding the composition of the piece. Your answers to these questions will serve as the first third of the paper, the *introduction:*

1. Find the Groves article about the composer and composition.
2. After reading the Groves article, select three entries from the bibliography at the end of the composer article, items which the Whitworth library holds.
3. Read the section in the articles or books pertaining to the composer's work on this particular composition.
4. Answer the following questions:
   a. Why was it written?
   b. From what part of the composer's creative life did this composition emerge?
   c. Why is the piece important to the twentieth century?
   Your answers to the above will serve as the first third of the paper, the introduction.

You are to turn in your first draft, the first two-thirds of the paper, no later than April 1.

Figure 7.1. Directions for the music assignment.

Figure 7.1 continued

Summary Activities:

Upon listening to the piece for the sixth time, you are to write the last third of your paper, answering the following question:

> *Thesis:* Listening to a musical composition repeatedly affects one's view of a composition in the following ways:

Your answer should address these additional questions:

1. What was the date of your sixth listening?
2. How does your current view of the composition differ from your first reaction?
3. Of what are you aware in the piece that was not evident the first time you listened?

Summarize the importance of the piece to you.

List at the end of the text all sources used in writing the paper. Include a bibliography (sources used in writing) and a discography (a list of the recordings used).

    In an appendix, list the dates of your second through fifth listenings. Tip: It is best to space the second through fifth listenings a week apart.

Student #1: I thought I would only respect this piece and never like it. Now I realize that I not only like this masterpiece, I am enamored [of] it. My ears have been converted to twentieth-century music. I should never listen to a composition and immediately make judgments. A lesson learned and wisdom gained through this assignment.

Student #2: If I ever got the chance, I would love to go and actually see the opera since I've seen it in my head so many times.

Student #3: Upon listening to [the piece] for the sixth time, I am convinced that listening to a musical composition repeatedly affects one's view of the music. From the first to the sixth listening, my recognition, appreciation, and understanding of the piece have changed considerably.

Student #4: After my first listening I concluded that I did not really like the work. . . . Now I can say that I have much respect for [the composer] and his masterpiece. . . . I truly enjoy the piece.

Student responses.

. . . . .

*Student
motivation
and learning.*

This is the most successful assignment in writing I have ever done. Students were motivated to a greater extent than in any other paper I have developed. There are still many small matters to refine in the assignment, but students were motivated to write, and they became very aware of the process of gaining appreciation and understanding of a new work.

Individual conferences will be held the next time the assignment is offered, Spring 1992.

[This professor wrote the above words in 1992. When we interviewed him in 1994, he was still using the assignment in essentially its original form. He had not yet held conferences; he was still writing his comments on the first draft. However, he again expressed his desire to hold conferences. Moreover, he gave us a fuller reflection on why this assignment had worked so well for him and his students: it had served as what he called a "carrying vehicle." Here are his words from the 1994 interview:]

*Learning: The
assignment
served as a
carrying
vehicle to
lead the
student to a
higher level of
understanding.*

*It makes the
class more
academic,
more serious.*

*Community:
feedback from
colleagues.*

*Good student
evaluations.*

You know, in music, the old cliché is you can lead a horse to water but you can't make him drink. We have to make 'em drink. And I think all of teaching is that way. This assignment is what you might call a carrying vehicle. It's a construct or a convention, a way that you develop in which students can be led to a higher level of understanding and knowledge. The first time you face it, people can resist it because it could look like busy work. Or they wonder why they have to do it. They have to have confidence in me that what they're going to arrive at is better. And all throughout music teaching I've had this. The old cliché is that you pass out a new piece of music to a band, and they don't like it at first, but it will be their favorite piece at the concert, once they have penetrated into the deeper meaning of the piece. And that's what I've done with this assignment. I have the students go beyond the veneer and penetrate into its greater depths, and they have greater knowledge of how it's organized and things like that. And it makes the class more academic, more serious. It's absolutely a beautiful assignment. I took it to a music meeting of the Christian College Coalition. I had thirty copies, and they were all gone in half a day. And I've gotten feedback from [names a colleague] at [names a college] in Iowa. She's adapted it a bit, but she still uses the basic idea. So I'm very pleased. . . . The other thing is, I just got the best set of evaluations I've ever gotten.

Strategies That Worked, #2

—Douglas Ross, International Business, TSU

[Note: In his 1994 interview, Ross, who had been involved in WAC since the 1980s, recounted strategies he had "tried in class and either kept or abandoned." This was one he had kept. In it, he divides the class into teams for business problem solving. Notice that this assignment involves no actual student writing, but the faculty member describes it as part of his growth through WAC and other experiences. It works for him because it enhances student learning, involvement, and community.]

A group exercise I've found fun to do and very, very rewarding is an exercise on crisis management. What I've done is to find several real situations that happened to companies. For example, a Baltimore manufacturer of peach preserves found that a piece of glass had gotten into one of its preserve bottles and cut a baby's lip. So what can you do with a situation like that?

Why it worked: I've found this exercise fun and rewarding.

Well, I form the class into teams, and these teams take the role of senior managers of a particular company. I give several different circumstances—not just peach preserves, but chemical spills, etc. Each of the teams has a different circumstance. I hand out the facts in several lines to this management team. Then I ask a series of questions: What do you need to know, where are you going to find the information, and what are you going to do about it? I give them ten minutes to discuss this.

I formed the class into teams taking the role of senior managers.

Then I'll say, "OK, there has been a new break in circumstances." So, I collect the first piece of paper and hand out the second, escalated set of circumstances. Instead of just the baby's lip being cut, now pieces of wood and everything else are turning up in their products, from Baltimore to Maine, that sort of thing. Again, the same three questions: What information do you need, where are you going to get it, and what are you going to do about it? And then more time, more discussion. All this is internal to each group.

I give them a crisis situation.

Then I walk around and say, OK, another escalation, and they all go, "Aaaah!" Welcome to the world.

At the end, I ask them to derive principles for dealing with crisis in a company.

In the debriefing time at the end, I ask them to set out answers to the three questions in relation to each group's circumstances. From those, we derive a series of principles for dealing with crisis in a company.

Now, an alternative course for me would be to stand up and say, "This is what you should do: look at the possible damage to the bottom line, guess what aspects of the

I could stand up and say, "This is what you should do." But, instead, I let them experience real circumstances.

organization are going to be affected," etc. But, instead, I let them experience very real circumstances from the perspective of a management team trying to deal with the circumstances and from there let them derive principles that they themselves think are going to be useful. That turns out to be a very potent exercise. They all remember it.

Strategies That Worked, #3
—Joseph Scanio, Physics, UC

[Note: Three years after his 1990 WAC workshop, Scanio contributed an article to the WAC Newsletter *at UC, describing his use of informal writing in large physics classes. The first section below is that article. The second section contains his reflections in 1995, when, as an associate dean, teaching a much reduced load, he reflected back on the strategy he had described. The assignment has worked for him because it is feasible even in a large class and, most of all, because it results in a kind of student learning he values very much.]*

I did not see how I could incorporate writing into my standard physics course.

At the workshop, it seemed like every ten minutes we were asked to write. The cumulative effect was quite remarkable.

I required five one-to-two-page writings during the quarter.

[From a 1993 UC *WAC Newsletter:*] It all began in the spring of 1990 at a one-hour, brown-bag WAC lunch meeting on campus. I did not see how I could possibly incorporate writing into my standard physics course, and I went to the meeting prepared to argue against writing in the sciences. There was nothing there for me, except for one concept which I had never considered before, that of informal writing: have the students write, not to be corrected and graded, but to enable the students to focus their ideas. I spent a fair amount of time mulling over how I might implement such an idea in my courses. Before I had time to formulate a new writing component to my courses, I attended a Shakertown WAC workshop later in 1990. There, it seemed that every ten minutes we were asked to write for ten or fifteen minutes on some subject. The cumulative effect of such writing was quite remarkable, and I was struck by how effective this was in organizing and expressing one's thoughts. I came home from Shakertown ready to try using informal writing.

I immediately implemented a writing component in the ninety-student introductory physics course in the spring and continued it during the following year in a special topics honors course in early universe cosmology. I required five one-to-two-page writings at two-week intervals during the quarter. The students were to write about anything "relevant" to the material being studied.

The papers had to be legible, and students were told they could be completed in under fifteen minutes. I did not grade the papers or correct grammar, spelling, or style. Course grades were completely determined by the "objective" components of the course: the problem sets, the tests, and the final exam. However, students who did not turn in all five writing assignments would receive an "I" grade. This would be changed to the earned letter grade if the student subsequently turned in the missing writings.

What, then, is the point? Having students hand in pages with words on them so that I can put five check marks by their names is hardly an exciting exercise. *It was absolutely crucial that I read the papers, make notes about them, and react to these papers in a directed way during the next class meeting.* The students would then be aware that I had actually read their specific papers, and if they included something of particular interest in their writings, I would comment about it. *The papers became progressively better through the quarter as students realized that I had actually taken time to read their writings.* While some students would give me matter-of-fact chapter summaries (which I believe were useful), most of them tried to produce an interesting anecdote. In fact, a student decided once to comment on the relevance and interest of each figure in a particular textbook chapter: this made me look at the figures in a totally new light!

The thousands of writing assignments I have read have convinced me that the students have been able to incorporate physics into their everyday thinking much more than they would have by merely doing the "objective" parts of the course. I have read many anecdotes with comments about how the student never realized before that there were physical laws governing the skidding of a car, an electrical shock, the rainbow he or she saw on the way to class, etc.

This writing component to my physics courses clearly requires time to read the papers and comment. However, since I am not grading or correcting them, I can read ninety papers in one to two hours. When I am using writing in two courses, I stagger the assignments. In addition, my reaction to the papers takes up class time, and I certainly cover less material now than I did before. This does not bother me in the least, since the class discussions we have while I am reacting to the writings are usually extremely useful in cementing concepts we have been discussing.

I did not grade the papers or correct grammar.

It was absolutely crucial that I read the papers and react to them at the next class meeting.

The papers became progressively better as the students realized I had read their writings.

Students have been able to incorporate physics into their everyday thinking.

Feasibility: I can read ninety papers in one to two hours.

I certainly cover less material now. That does not bother me in the least since class discussions now are extremely useful in cementing concepts.

Has student performance improved as a result of this writing component to the courses? I do not know. The averages on the exams have not changed. Nevertheless, the writing is another way in which the students can interact with physics, and, in that sense, I believe it is beneficial. I have read many writings that begin with a statement about not understanding a certain concept, and then, as the writing proceeds, the student begins to realize what is happening, and, by the end, he or she rephrases the concept in a way that indicates that a creative thought process has occurred.

The Future: I intend to continue this informal writing in any elementary course I teach. I am convinced that the students do learn from the exercise, as long as they hand in the writings on time. Occasionally, a student will come to the final exam with all five writing assignments and tell me how painful it is to do all five at once.

The writing is another way for students to interact with physics.

What else can be done? I would like to find a way to introduce writing in our large (550-student) calculus-based introductory course. The standard complaint from students is that they cannot do the problems. If they were asked to write down what it is about the problem that they cannot do, then they might be able to focus their thoughts and actually go a long way toward solving the problem on their own. If and when I teach this course again, I shall contemplate how to digest 550 daily or weekly thoughts on why students have trouble with physics problems.

A creative thought process has occurred.

·   ·   ·   ·

[The following are his reflections in 1995. He has become associate dean of Arts and Sciences:]

I intend to continue this informal writing.

Yes, I still use basically the same technique. It's still fun; it still works. I don't teach calculus now, so I haven't integrated the journal there as I said I would. But I use it in an honors course on the first five seconds of the universe. There, the journals are different. Not so much describing car crashes, but more "I didn't understand Chapter 2." That's because the topic of the course is more divorced from real life.

Strategies That Worked, #4
—Carl Huether, Biology, UC

[Note: In this 1996 interview, seven years after his first WAC workshop, Huether describes an assignment in a large biology class where students, on e-mail, respond to articles about biological topics. His ways of making large classes interactive are featured in a thirty-minute faculty-development video, Making Large Classes Interactive, *produced in 1996 at the University of Cincinnati. The video has won two national awards. (See works cited list.)]*

Five years ago, I began teaching a large biology class for nonscience majors. The challenge was how to get the 400 students involved in the learning process. So I tried extra credit projects. One of them is the electronic journal on the network. The students buy, in the bookstore, a packet which contains instructions and the six scientific articles to which they must respond. Students are assigned to their own personal accounts on the e-mail. Students are arranged in groups of ten to fifteen. Then they read the articles and respond to four of the six. Those responses are circulated to the ten or fifteen other students in their group. The other students are required, in turn, to give six additional responses to the additional responses. So each student winds up giving four initial responses and six secondary responses for a total of ten. The teaching assistants (five are assigned to the course) evaluate the responses and assign credit.

The students clearly learn a lot about science. But, also, it's a wonderful opportunity for students to get to know the e-mail system. They can now communicate with anyone in the world. We have about 30–40 percent of the students participating in this extra-credit project.

In science, we are trained in research and scholarship but not trained in how to become educators. So when we get here, it takes a long time to learn. I got my initial view of students as clients or customers in my position as director of the program in genetic counseling. We spend a lot of time worrying about our clients. As I thought about my own educational position here, I thought, "Why shouldn't we see students in the same way?"

Complex Stories: Strategies That Worked, Strategies That Didn't, and Why

The next section contains some longer, more complex stories, so that readers can see how the strategies that worked and those that didn't work are typically intermingled in a faculty member's experience.

"What Works, That's the Main Thing"
—Sociology, UC

[Note: This faculty member teaches sociology in three different settings: the College of Evening and Continuing Studies and the Institute for Learning in Retirement, both at UC, and also a graduate-level theological seminary.

The interview, in 1994, three years after his WAC workshop at UC, shows how enormously different his three teaching situations appear to him and how he varies his teaching strategies to accommodate them. He is aware of the enormously diverse factors that affect his classrooms—economic constraints (students at UC must retain a certain grade-point average for their employers to keep paying their tuition), physical constraints of class size (forty at UC, eight to fifteen at the seminary), and students' language backgrounds.

His story also reveals some of the criteria he uses to make decisions about what is working. Getting students involved in the community of the classroom is highly important to him, and he struggles hard to achieve it. In his view, informal writing works because it has provided a significant new way to create that community he desires. But even his best strategy for getting students involved—in-class writing—does not work in all of his teaching situations.

He gives a mixed report on peer collaboration. On the one hand, what he calls "peer editing" is one of his first and most vivid memories about the Shakertown workshop, and he thinks it's "a good model." On the other hand, he says he doesn't use it. Then he describes how he does use it, but only for formal papers. Formal papers, it seems to him, are not really WAC—an example of the difficulty with defining WAC which we discussed earlier in this chapter.

The interview took place in 1994, four years after the faculty member had attended a two-day WAC workshop. The interviewer is Virginia Slachman, then a graduate assistant at UC.]

Peer editing at the workshop was a good model, but I don't use it.

Interviewer: What do you remember about the workshop?

Faculty: The peer editing. We would read things to another person and get feedback and then go back and rewrite. And then I think sometimes we would read the edited version to the total group and then have open discussion in the whole group.

Interviewer: Did that seem like a good model?

Faculty: Yes, that was a good model.

Interviewer: Was that something you used after that?

Faculty: Uh, no, not the peer editing.

Interviewer: What impacted the way you taught after the workshop?

Faculty: What I got out of it is, forget about grammar and structure and all the formal, intimidating aspects of writing and just write, using simple language, and also write under pressure at times. In my classes, I say, "OK, folks, write for three minutes. I prefer that you use full sentences, but if you want to use clauses, that's OK. You don't have to worry about paragraph structure. I won't keep these; I'll give them back to you."

What I got out of it: just write.

I ask open-ended statements: just, "What does this say?" "What problems do you see here?" "What does this mean?" "How do you feel about this?" "What do you think about this?"

How I use in-class writing.

At the university, oh, let's say I had forty students in a class. At the seminary, I have small groups, eight to fifteen. But the methodology would be the same. Except, at the university, I *collected* the papers, without names on them. I shuffled them and then handed them out, and then we read them and we discussed. Naturally, at the university, we didn't have time to discuss all the papers. At the seminary, we did.

Adapting in-class writing to different settings.

It was a little bit frustrating because we dragged that part of the class on too long. But they didn't have confidence in what they were saying; they edited as they went along. And I wanted them to have their first thoughts.

Frustrations of in-class writing: the time it takes, students' lack of confidence.

I would say that the chief contribution of WAC is, when you face a group and you put a question to them or you make some kind of a leading provocative statement, two or three people will respond. The large block of people will be passive. And I'm accustomed to looking at them with almost tears in my eyes: please participate, please participate—save me and save the class. This way [with the writing], everybody's thinking about it. They're engaged. Like it or not, you got 'em hooked.

Why in-class writing works: engagement and community.

Oh, by the way, I've also taught at the Institute for Learning in Retirement. That would be more creative. For example, I gave them a definition of a concept called "metanarrative." Metanarrative is a brief statement about yourself, who you are. I gave that as homework. They brought it back the following week. A couple of them were so good I had them reprinted in the informational bulletin of the Institute for Learning.

Another is, at the Institute for Learning, I teach a course on the Hebrew prophets. So we were reading Isaiah and Jeremiah and all these people, and I gave them a modern

The basic principle: It's the writing, you see.

update: "What if a prophet appeared in Fountain Square [downtown plaza, frequent site of demonstrations in Cincinnati]? What would he say about the sins of Cincinnati or the sins of the U.S.? Would you please write a prophecy?" That was not under the pressure of time. But it's the writing, you see; this is what they drilled into us at the workshop.

Before the workshop, I had never done this before in my life. I began like any other teacher: "The subject for today is race relations in Cincinnati, and here are some interesting things" or "Have you ever had any experiences with hostility on the job?" [Students would say,] "Oh, job. What was it? Well, I don't, mmmm, uh." I always had the burden of lifting them up, and I'm tired of lifting them up and then praying to God that somebody's going to get interested. I would go into a mild panic. It's not quite panic, but it's unpleasant, to push, to push, to push, because their minds are somewhere else. About what's going to be on the exam. That's all the students want to know: What's going to be on the exam. I've had people follow me out to my car in the parking lot, arguing with me about their grades or their assignments.

Why in-class writing works: community.

Interviewer: Does that happen at the seminary?

Faculty: Oh, no, that doesn't happen at the seminary. I don't have to give exams here. We have pass-fail here. No, that mentality is over at the university. I taught in the evening college, where, if your grades fall below a certain average, the company doesn't pay for the tuition, so there's a lot of money riding on that.

· · · ·

Where in-class writing doesn't work. Reason: manipulation destroys community.

Over here at the seminary, after the second time I used in-class writing with a particular class, they felt, "Okay, you're manipulating us." They don't want to do that anymore. Also, I think in-class writing has to be used sparingly. I don't believe an instructor should start every class this way. I think you shoot your wad—you've blown it. What works, that's the main thing.

· · · ·

Interviewer: You said that you don't use peer collaboration.

I use peer collaboration, but that's not WAC.

Faculty: No, I don't have time for that. I'm not teaching writing. I do use peer collaboration, but that's nothing to do with WAC. For example, I have a course here where people write papers, but that's not WAC; that's more traditional. They [photocopy] the papers, and they hand them out in the class, and the assignment for the whole class is to read those papers—not to critique them but to respond to them—and then the next class day we would respond to them, so that's the "peer" there. That's a course in human relations. To get this really tightly drawn, I would say, submit a trial outline of your paper. Submit a trial bibliography. And then I would use peer involvement: "What do you think of the issues being raised here?"

Interviewer: How did that work?

Faculty: Oh, that works pretty well. But I wouldn't do that at the university.

Interviewer: Why not?

Faculty: Well, evening college people are tired, and the logistics of it would be overwhelming, to try to get peer collaboration. Well, you could do it by having groups of two. But, as you know very well, there's a decline in the art of writing and a resistance, strong resistance, to writing. And also people can't put sentences together anymore, even here at the seminary, and this is a school that is five years beyond the bachelor of arts degree. I've had people sit in that chair and show me a sermon or something like that [that was], in two words, as my father likes to say, "not possible."

> *Peer collaboration cannot be used at the university. Reason: logistics, community, feasibility.*

"So in That Class, It Seemed to Work Pretty Well"
—Criminal Justice, UC

[Note: This interview took place in 1994, four years after the faculty member had attended a WAC workshop. The interviewer is Virginia Slachman, then a graduate assistant in the WAC office at UC. The faculty member's story shows how keenly she strives for good relations with her students and how much her definition of what works depends upon what students respond to favorably, what helps her create community, with and among her students, and what enhances learning.]

Faculty: I teach courses on sexual assault and rape, race, etc. The classes are sixty to eighty students. When I started teaching "Race, Class, and Crime" seven years ago, it was real hard to deal with race *in the criminal justice system* when most of the whites in the class hadn't even thought about their *own* racism. The class just did not work for the first few years, and I was real frustrated. I mean, it worked for some of the students, but a lot of them just hated it, and

> *The class just did not work before WAC.*

> *The problem: racial tension.*

there'd be frustrating tensions between the black and white students. So I went to RAPP, the Racial Awareness Pilot Project on campus. One of the things that they gave me was three questions: (1) When were you first aware of racism? (2) What messages did you get when you were growing up about different races? And (3) how do those messages affect you today? RAPP developed the three questions, but I didn't see them as a useful writing assignment until I went to Shakertown. I had done them just as a discussion. After Shakertown, I saw them as a springboard to get students to write.

Using writing to address racial tension. The payoff: student learning. Reading the papers was incredible.

So I gave students a take-home writing assignment to answer the three questions. And I did grade these. Some of the students didn't take it seriously at all and would write a few sentences on each one. But most of the students really put a lot of thought into it. Reading through them was incredible. I would look for patterns and make a lot of comments on them and talk about them the next week. For example, I would say, "Look how many of you wrote that your parents were not racist as far as going to a school that was integrated, but a lot of you said if you went to a dance with somebody of a different race, especially if you were white, then all of a sudden it was different." Then we can look at these scales of racism. So going to Shakertown really helped me to develop those kinds of things. One of the things I learned at Shakertown was that if you have people do a writing assignment before they do a discussion, then the quiet people will be more likely to talk.

Community: the quiet people will talk.

Interviewer: Did you find that to be true?

Faculty: Yes, definitely. They had something there to look at, and they had thought it through, and they didn't feel the lack of confidence and shyness. It also gave them the feeling it was OK to talk about their own racism or to question things. It brought up some heated arguments in the class, and I used to hate those, and I'm still not comfortable with them, but I think they're useful learning exercises for everybody. And I just tell everybody, "As long as everybody is respectful when they're asking and answering questions, then that's why we're here."

Move from open-ended to more structured assignments. Writing works because it is manageable in the available time. Result: more students are reading.

Another thing I changed after the Shakertown workshop: rather than saying, "Just tell me what you're thinking about what you're learning in this class," I give them a particular question that is related to the readings and to what I've lectured about. So it's sort of like I'm giving an essay question. But on the exam, if I have them do essay questions with eighty students, I'd never get them graded. But this way, I just have one question that I do for a little over half the class sessions of the quarter. I allow them to drop their lowest grade, but if they miss a class, then they can't make it up. I still haven't quite worked it all out, but it seems to be working all right. One thing I found [was] that many more of them started doing the reading than before.

And the other thing was, just in the last couple of years, I've noticed that they have really liked the idea that I thought of them as critical thinkers, which I did not communicate to them before.

Interviewer: How did you discover that?

Faculty: They always liked that I wrote a lot of comments on their reaction papers. But there were some students in there who never spoke, who did OK on multiple-choice exams, but wrote these incredible critiques of the readings. I didn't always agree with them, but they were very good.

I always told them, "I don't agree with you, but it's very well written and it's an 'A+' paper." Typically, the first couple of times I do that in the class, I make a copy of some of the best ones and hand them out to the whole class and say, "This is what I'm looking for." I started showing them that I valued the [notion] that they could critique something and that they could be critical thinkers. And when I saw that they liked that—and, again, not for every student, but for a significant portion of them—then I started at the beginning of the quarter by saying, "I want you to be critical thinkers. You don't just come to college to input, input, input. You need to be processing what you're inputting, because I know as well as you do that you're not hearing the same thing in all of your classes. You may hear in my class that we have a very unjust criminal justice system, and I know you're hearing in your other classes that things are very fair. And you have to think about what you're reading and what you're learning. Because, obviously, you're getting a lot of different messages. And you don't need to think of this just in terms of who's right, but what do you think? How does this make sense? What are some of the potential flaws in it?" And they really responded to that.

And what's been interesting, and I guess surprising to me, is that the undergraduates seem to respond much better than the graduate students.

Students really liked the idea that I treated them as critical thinkers.

And when I saw they liked that, I started at the beginning of the quarter by saying, "I want you to be critical thinkers." They really responded to that.

Interviewer: Why?

Faculty: I don't know. A lot of times, when I try to do freewrites or things like that, even though the next year they might tell me, "Oh, I decided I did like that," at the time they were real resistant to it. They felt it was just busy work, that I was just doing that instead of giving lectures. They wanted . . . real in-depth discussions in class, and yet I've had a real hard time getting those discussions going. One of the problems is that grad classes are two hours. If I had to pick my greatest frustration and the things I'm worst at with WAC, it would be using it in a graduate class.

Last year, I did [teach] a really wonderful grad class that was an elective, . . . the best one I've taught since I've been here. Interestingly, it only had one criminal justice major in it. It was a very hard class. They had to read a whole lot, and they had a two-page paper due every week. I sometimes had them do informal writings in there, which [they] seemed to like. But the weekly two-page paper had to be scholarly. They could not use the word "I." They were not to use personal experiences anymore. I started with twenty students, and ten of them dropped it after the first week when they saw it was a lot of reading and a lot of writing. At first I was—I'm still—irritated by that. I was disappointed because I thought, "Oh this is too bad, that grad students are that lazy." And I tried to just say, "Well, maybe they had a statistics course this quarter, and they felt they just couldn't put that much time into it." But it was a good class, and those students got a lot of my feedback. Every week I graded the two-page papers very specifically, very rigorously, I carefully graded them within twenty-four hours, I had everybody's home address, and I mailed them to them right away so that they would have [their paper] before they had to write the next one. Then, in addition, for about the first half of the quarter, I would type up summaries of common mistakes or things to think about. For example, I talked about using the word "Americans" to mean people from the U.S. So let's think about that, and I've had to train myself. It wasn't always grammatical or stylistical, although most of them tended to be. So, in that class, that seemed to work pretty well. It finally got to the point where they seemed to know pretty much what I wanted. They got very good at integrating the reading with their writing. After a while, I still mailed them the feedback, but I did not have to do the summaries.

Freewrites have not worked well in graduate classes. Students were resistant.

One grad class worked well. They had two-page papers due.

They liked the informal writing.

But it was a good class, and students got a lot of my feedback.

Responding to students' writing.

So in that class it seemed to work pretty well.

Result: better student work.

When I got my end-of-quarter student evaluations, about three of the ten wrote that they were rather put out that I had not allowed them to use personal pronouns or personal experiences in the two-page papers. And one or two of them said they felt that that meant they couldn't critique it. So one of the things I realized . . . was that the next time I teach using that method, I'm going to have to communicate to [students] that just because you're summarizing the readings and I don't like you to use the word "I" or your personal experience, that doesn't mean you can't critique what you're reading. And you can use your personal experiences during class. What I'm trying to do is to get them to see that when you write for professional journals, you're not going to be using your personal experience.

Interviewer: You said, in general, that your grad classes don't work.

Faculty: Right. Sometimes I think it's the quality of the grad students. There were a lot of them who weren't doing the writings. Many of them would, in fact, be quite hostile on the teaching evaluations. They saw this as babysitting them and checking that they had done the readings. Well, that was partly true, and I'm not going to apologize for that, either, because my experience has been that a lot of them *don't* do the readings. What happens is, I'll discuss the readings during lecture or we'll have a class discussion, and a lot of them will just bank on the fact that they're going to find out what was in the readings so they don't have to do them, and they'll know what I think is important in order to answer the exam.

Interviewer: It seems there were some specific things suggested at Shakertown which you implemented, and some of those which you had to continue to refine.

Faculty: Right, and I'm still refining them, that's very true. One of the things that I was already doing, which, until Shakertown, I didn't realize anybody else did except for me, was allowing them to hand papers in early and grading them and then giving them back. That's a really great idea, because otherwise you spend all this time writing comments and correcting somebody's paper. And, of course, the worst papers are the ones you spend the most time on, and those tend to be the students that don't come and pick the papers up anyway. And I hate editing other people's work; I absolutely just loathe it. I don't even like

Next time I have to communicate to them.

Grad students saw this as babysitting.

I'm still refining.

Draft response works because your communication to students is used.

Some of them will take the feedback seriously.

doing my own, but I really hate doing other people's. So, to me, that was incredibly frustrating. But with the research methods class, which I taught both undergrad and grad, I make them design a research model. They have to come up with what would be your hypothesis, and given this hypothesis what are your dependent and independent variables, what's your sample going to be. Some people have a very hard time formulating that. If I let them hand in an idea to me, and I give them some feedback, some of them will really take that feedback very seriously and turn a "D" paper into an "A" paper, not just changing with my feedback, but taking it extra steps beyond that.

Interviewer: Have you used peer collaboration?

I haven't used peer collabo-ration.

Faculty: I really haven't. The only thing, I had lunch with Barbara Walvoord and somebody from the sociology department—I've forgotten his name; somebody I hadn't met before—and peer collaboration was supposed to be what we talked about, and that was kind of helpful. I can't remember exactly what I got out of it, but I can remember thinking when I left the lunch that it had been helpful.

Interviewer: What stands out most to you about Shakertown?

It was okay if the ideas didn't work.

Faculty: The validation of the importance of teaching and trying different methods to teach something and that it was OK if they didn't work.

"There Were a Lot of Good Ideas I Didn't Use"
—John Yoder, Political Science and History, Whitworth

[Note: The interviewer is Linda Hunt. The interview was conducted in 1994, five years after Yoder's first WAC workshop. It illustrates how a faculty member uses WAC to build what he believes are his own personal strengths, deliberately ignoring other aspects. The story also contains a marvelous account of the difficulties of using journals in a multicultural learning environment. Figure 7.2 is a copy of Yoder's assignment sheet for the research paper.]

I realized my work wasn't as productive as it could have been.

Interviewer: What happened in the workshop?

Faculty: Well, I think I came away recognizing that I'd always put in a lot of work teaching writing, and much of that work wasn't as productive as it could have been, and maybe it was misdirected. And I also learned there are ways of teaching students the skills that go into writing.

Prior to the workshop, what I had done was take a paper and virtually rewrite it for the student, which is maybe not such a bad idea, although I think I was a bit heavy-handed, and the process was excessively time-consuming. But I didn't have any accountability afterwards. I just handed the corrected papers back to the students and expected that would do some good. And, once in a while, I'd come back in the fall and see the papers still in the box, and even *I* had to admit that if the students didn't bother to pick up the papers, my method probably wasn't doing a lot of good.

Interviewer: What kinds of changes did you initiate after the workshop?

Faculty: Well, there were a lot of good ideas that I didn't use. As Barbara [Walvoord] kept saying, "You can only use so many things." And my goal is to teach students how to do a good research project. That's probably what I myself do best. And I think that's critical for graduate school or for their professional work. And so I put together a package: steps to produce a research project. And in some ways it was modeled on one of Barbara's presentations. She described a professor who had devised a scheme to help students do research. I used that a bit, but I basically thought back, "How do *I* put together a research project?" And I broke that process down into steps. This method teaches not just how to write but how to approach a project, how to develop a question, how to become familiar with the basic literature, how to organize, and how to collect data. I put all those items together in steps, culminating in a rough draft that I read and turn back to the students, and then a final draft incorporating my comments. So I think this process broke everything down into steps and provided accountability.

There were a lot of good ideas that I didn't use.

Guiding the research paper.

Draft responses.

Interviewer: And did you conference that first draft? I thought you described to me once that you had conferences.

Faculty: Yes, I did, and I still do sometimes, but not as frequently. I'm always torn among the multiple goals I have for each class, and I've got a lot of material in courses. To do conferencing means basically I must give up one week of classes. So now I don't drop class. Students schedule meetings with me and come in. Probably half the students come in.

Problem: logistics and coverage.

Some students complain about my detailed formula for writing papers. And I'm sure it may hurt my teacher

---

Guide for the Research Project

Preparing a successful research paper is a complex but not impossible task. While cramming for an exam may be somewhat like running the 100-meter dash, writing a research paper is more like completing a marathon. Students who pace themselves and who plan their efforts carefully will do far better than students who expend brilliant but short bursts of energy. In writing a paper, as in running a long-distance race, the secret is preparation and persistence.

During the course of the semester, you will complete all of the steps essential for writing a journal-length article. Because the steps are cumulative, it is necessary to take them in sequence, and it is critical that you proceed in a timely manner. Therefore, each of the following assignments is due at the start of the class period designated in the syllabus. Projects turned in after the start of that class period will receive reduced credit. And, because all projects are sequential, I will not accept any subsequent project until you have completed the previous assignment.

Except where specifically indicated, all assignments must be typed, and they must be kept together in a labeled file folder or note-card packet.

Step One: Background Reading

In preparation for choosing your research topic, scan a number of journals and read several general essays about an area of interest to you. Tables of contents and articles in journals or introductory chapters in current books provide a quick overview and help identify the most basic issues and arguments of concern for scholars. These materials will also refer to the most essential sources and the most important scholars working on the topics you may wish to research.

For your folder, submit one or two pages listing titles, authors' names, and the dates of the sources you read. Also list the major points covered in the essays, any problems, arguments, or debates you encountered (these are often good research topics), and a short list of key sources noted in the essays. (10 points, due February 19.)

Step Two: A Key Question

Research papers attempt to answer an important question; they do not just summarize information. Once the question has been formulated clearly and precisely, the rest of your task is to gather data and develop logical arguments which will answer the question. In a completed research paper, the answer to this question is the thesis statement.

For your folder, submit a research question of no more than one paragraph. (5 points, due February 28.)

Step Three: Web of Ideas

In preparation for your library work, you need to identify the key issues which relate to your question. These issues or topics can be linked together in a weblike structure that is a primitive outline. The advantages of a web are that the web may be expanded or modified easily and that the web provides a visual representation of the logic of your argument. [Inserts boxed item

Figure 7.2. History course guide for the research project.

Figure 7.2 continued

---

illustrating web.]

For your folder, submit a one-page handwritten web of ideas. (10 points, due March 7.)

Step Four: Annotated Bibliography

Good research is based on a careful survey of existing primary and secondary data. Secondary works contain the observations, judgments, and conclusions of other scholars, while primary data are the raw materials which you may use to build your own argument.

For your folder, submit a two- to three-page alphabetized, annotated bibliography. The annotation should indicate the general nature of the material contained in the work and an indication of the author's perspective. If possible, two works should be primary sources. (10 points, due March 14.)

Step Five: Notes on Reading and Research

Using 3 x 5 cards, keep a careful record of your sources and of the information you gather during your research process. The cards need not be typed, but they should conform to the following model: [inserts boxes illustrating cards].

For your folder, submit one bibliography card and one note card (either a summary or a quote). (5 points, due March 14 with annotated bibliography.)

Step Six: Outline

Having completed all the previous steps, you are now ready to prepare a detailed outline of your essay. The outline should begin with a thesis statement (the now-answered question).

For your folder, submit a two- or three-page outline. Organize your note cards according to the section of your outline, and with a red pen write the appropriate outline number on the cards you will use in writing a paper. (10 points, due April 17.)

Step Seven: Rough Draft

A successful paper must always go through several drafts that are revised and improved. Because the first draft is not a polished piece of work, it is not important to correct spelling or grammatical errors. It is important, however, to use the draft to get comments from other readers. It is also important that the rough draft uses complete and standard footnoting for documenting quotations and ideas.

For your folder, submit a complete rough draft (computer printout) of your paper. To the draft, attach the signed comments of at least two other people who have read your paper. (15 points, due April 23.)

Step Eight: Final Draft

The final draft of any paper is a carefully crafted piece of writing, free of spelling and grammatical errors. The point of the paper should be very clear to the reader, and you should never expect the reader to search between the lines to untangle the message you intend the paper to convey.

Figure 7.2 continued

> For your folder, submit a final revision of the draft prepared for step seven. I will make no corrections on the paper, but I will not assign a grade to any paper with five or more spelling errors, five or more major grammatical errors, or a combination of seven or more spelling and grammatical errors. Papers containing the above number of errors will be returned, and you must correct the problems before you can receive any credit. For my definition of a major error, refer to numbers 2, 3, 4, 5, 6, and 8 in "Guidelines for Writing Papers." [Guidelines not included here.] (20 points, due May 7.)

Students complain, but I don't get bad papers anymore.

evaluations a bit. But I've noticed that I don't get bad papers anymore. Also, students do a lot more reading for their papers. They do a lot more reflective thinking. And even though I don't conference as intentionally, students still come in and talk to me about their papers, or they'll talk to me after class.

An international student: "This is very different."

I had an international student, a really ambitious student, who, after the second week of class, said, "Well, I'm on my final draft." Then I said, "Let's look at the steps for doing research that I've outlined in the syllabus." And he wasn't real happy about that at first. But then, a week later, he came and said, "I really want to learn how to write a paper. I realize this is very different than anything I've done." He's from Kenya, and he wanted to do his paper in African history, which is an area where I can work with him very closely.

· · · ·

Interviewer: Have you used in-class writes?

I have not used in-class writes. Reasons: feasibility, logistics, community: getting the writing back.

Faculty: That I don't do. Two reasons. One is—and maybe I don't do it right—in-class writes can be very time-consuming if I have to read them and grade them or anything like that. Ideally, I would like to give pop quizzes every week, just to keep students up to speed. But I virtually have given up on that just because the ungraded papers pile up on my desk. And getting work back quickly is so important. The other thing, most of my courses are pretty content oriented. And so it might be a bit harder, though not impossible, to devise an in-class writing.

For me, it's basically a question of time. I'm probably like other people: I heard lots of ideas at the workshop, and the ideas I heard that seemed most important to me were related to doing the research project. And maybe if I went back and looked at my workshop material, some other ideas would be there, and I'd say, "Oh, those would really be helpful and good." And they probably just sort of faded from my memory.

Interviewer: How about journals with travel? Have you done those?

Faculty: Yes, and that is very helpful. We took a group to South Africa, and students wrote a journal. Earlier, when I was in Liberia, I had followed the model much more closely. I had a list of topics to guide students in producing a journal. Unfortunately, that got me in trouble politically. My list of topics got clear to the president's mansion [laughs].

Interviewer: Because?

Faculty: The year before, there had been an American girl at the same school. She had kept a journal like other American kids do. Some of her African roommates got hold of her journal and read it. It said some things that weren't terribly complimentary to the president of the country. Privacy is not nearly as important as dignity in Africa. As a result, in a few days the contents of that journal were known in the executive mansion in Monrovia, a hundred and twenty kilometers away. When I got to the university, they said, "Are you going to have your students write journals?" Being honest, I said, "Yes." When they wondered what we were going to write about, I gave them my list of topics. And the next day the president of the university and all of his cabinet called me into the president's office to explain my project. They also listed the topics they didn't want the students to write about. In addition, they wanted permission to read the journals afterward. [Laughs] I mean, they were scared. And the president said, "Look, you know, we get money from the state, and if we embarrass the president or cause trouble, this could jeopardize our funding; it could jeopardize the status of the university." And so we sort of worked out a compromise. I knocked out some of the topics that, to them, would have seemed embarrassing.

· · · · ·

Certainly the writing workshop was pivotal.

Interviewer: And why would that be?

Faculty: To me, teaching writing is just critically important. One of the things I've said over and over is that we

I heard lots of ideas at the workshop and chose the most important to me.

Journals have been very helpful with students on field trips.

In Liberia, the journal got me in trouble.

The workshop was pivotal.

We err on the side of good teaching rather than good learning.

I'm going to err on the side of helping students learn, although it's easy to slip back.

have to be far more concerned that students learn than that we're good teachers. And I think, at Whitworth, at times, we err on the side of good teaching rather than good learning. We emphasize delivery and how things are presented, and that doesn't necessarily translate into the students' really understanding and learning the material, grappling with the material. That can be hard and frustrating at times, although I think in the end it pays off tremendously. Presenting a well-designed, tight lecture is fun, and it's beautiful, but it may not always be compatible with student learning. And I'm going to always, I hope, err on the side of helping students learn, although it's easy to slip back into the presenting mode.

A Divergent Voice

"Has It Influenced My Teaching? Well, I Can't Put My Finger on Anything Specific"
—History, TSU

[Note: This Towson State professor, during a ten-year period, has taught writing-intensive courses and attended several WAC workshops of various types and lengths. He has served on a WAC committee and has been a regular member of the Faculty Writers' Response Group, where faculty respond to one another's writing. Dowling observed his class, talked to his students, and worked with him. The interview was conducted in 1994. The interviewer was Dowling.

The faculty member claims not to have been influenced by WAC. But listen carefully to this voice. Note the strong connection between the Faculty Writers' Response Group, which gave him the valuable and thorough criticism he'd not gotten elsewhere, and his teaching philosophy—lots of criticism is good for students. Criticism, expressed as red marks on the exams, seems, for him, to be the basis for community, an act of caring, not hostility. Those who criticized him for the red marks, he thinks, have themselves neglected the thing that students and writers need most—thorough, rigorous criticism. And to slavishly copy the critiquer's corrections, as he says his students do, rather than productively using the critique, is a betrayal of community. It renders draft response for him a frustrating and ineffective method for helping students. Further, in his view, the role of content knowledge in thinking is extremely important. That belief shapes much of his approach to teaching and writing. This faculty member is not resisting WAC, in his own mind. The converts have his blessing. He assigns and critiques lots of writing in his classes. He's *given hours and hours of his time in the service of WAC—but he maintains the right to be "old-fashioned," to guide his teaching by his own philosophy, and to take or ignore WAC strategies, given his theoretical base, his time constraints, and his own experiences as a writer.]*

Faculty: Back in the early days of the writing group [TSU faculty who met to respond to one another's writing], much of what we did was creative writing.

The faculty writing group.

Interviewer: You were doing poems in those days. One or two eventually got published.

Faculty: Yes, and I eventually got two articles published. I remember I gave the group a sketch for a novel, with a few scenes in detail. We kicked that around, and I couldn't get across to the group that this was not a final product. I just wanted to find out whether this was psychologically a sound plot. But much of what they did was helpful. My previous novel was much improved by the group's comments. My agent had worked with me, but the writing group is the first time I'd gotten really sustained comment. It never bothered me to get criticism.

It never bothered me to get criticism.

Interviewer: Did the writing group carry over to your classroom?

Faculty: Has it influenced my way of teaching? Well, I can't put my finger on anything specific. Some aspects of style.

Interviewer: I remember, in 1984, you presented an exam paper to a writing workshop.

Faculty: Yes, I had red ink all over the student's paper. I have this compulsion to correct students when they're wrong, and I think that helps them. If we put it off, that doesn't help. That's why they come to college not knowing—because other teachers have put it off. In the workshop, I really got jumped on. But those were a bunch of education people who don't really believe in criticizing students very rigorously.

I think correcting students helps them.

　　Draft response is good in theory, but I have such a paper load, I can't do it. Also, I end up just grading myself, because the students just copy the corrections I've made. They don't think it through on their own.

　　I do give my 290 class the option of rewriting their prospectus. I presented that at a workshop one time—how I get my history students to write a prospectus for their term papers.

Draft response is good in theory, but I can't do it. Students just copy the corrections I've made.

I don't do
journals
either, because
of time.

I don't do journals, either, because of lack of time. Those might work well in English or health sciences. In history, I'm not sure it's very relevant. I'm very old-fashioned. In my department, our feeling is that students can't think if they don't have anything to think about. At first we have to teach them stuff, and then later they can mull it over.

Some of the people I've met in WAC seem almost to have had a religious conversion. That was great. But I wonder if we're fighting a losing battle, with computers, and psychologists telling us we can do as well with objective tests.

·   ·   ·   ·

WAC is
writing in
essay form.

Interviewer: How would you define WAC?

Faculty: WAC is writing in an essay-like form.

·   ·   ·   ·

Interviewer: Do you talk about teaching with colleagues in your department?

Faculty: A typical conversation in my department goes like this: we in history grade essays and book reports; we do nothing else from September until May. And these other featherbedders only have objective exams, so of course they can publish more [laughs].

Each of these very different faculty stories shows WAC as part of a complex mosaic that includes faculty members' own experiences as writers, their deeply held beliefs about teaching, their departmental contexts, their teaching loads, their personal styles, and their approaches to risk and change. While faculty were not always sure whether a strategy was "WAC," they focused on what "works." They asked whether a strategy would help to achieve community, whether it would enhance student learning, whether it was feasible, and whether it fit their own philosophies, priorities, and styles of teaching. But most of all, what emerged for us from all these faculty stories was the sense of faculty as active constructors of their own meanings, as changers and searchers, each struggling to find a self, to help learners, to develop community.

8 WAC and Faculty Career Patterns

WAC changed my life.
    —Sociology, UC

Beyond looking at faculty's teaching philosophies, attitudes, and strategies, we examined our data for evidence about WAC's impact on faculty members' broader professional lives and career patterns.

WAC did not occur in a vacuum for our faculty. It was part of a rich mix of ongoing experiences and changes. Faculty journeys were marked by periods of rapid change and periods of fallow, periods of frustration and periods of exhilaration. The journeys they recounted were shaped by their own personalities—we had tortoises and hares, introverts and extroverts, optimists and pessimists. But mostly we just had *people* in all their complexity, all their variety. And WAC had been part of their journey.

We were especially struck by the fact that WAC took its place among a wide variety of other development experiences—a seminar in syllabus design, help from a spouse, a critical-thinking workshop, a discussion with colleagues, a team-teaching experience, a particularly meaningful encounter with a student, a graduate school experience vividly recalled. The WAC experience blended with all of these others. Sometimes our respondents could not exactly pin down whether a development had arisen from a WAC workshop. Once again, we were reminded that the boundaries of WAC are more distinct to us as WAC professionals than they were to the faculty we studied.

Amid this diversity, however, we identified six themes that occurred in faculty's career development relative to WAC. These themes are not mutually exclusive, and one individual's account may exhibit several themes.

This chapter briefly discusses and illustrates the six themes; it then presents a collection of faculty members' narratives that illustrate those themes.

1. The Road Not Taken

One path was for faculty to become increasingly involved in educational reform to which WAC was seen as peripheral. For example, in recent years, mathematicians at the University of Cincinnati have become heavily involved in the significant reforms their department is undertaking to make undergraduate education more interactive, collaborative, and effective, and to integrate technology such as the graphing calculator into students' learning. Both of the UC mathematicians we interviewed in 1994 credited WAC with having been, in a vague sense, an impetus for their interest in reform. But they also separated themselves from WAC in significant ways. They saw WAC as having been peripheral to this math reform, to their discipline, and sometimes to their respective teaching styles. One math faculty member said:

> There are a number of discipline-specific reform movements in math. In this department, the revitalizing of our teaching by writing has been left behind by most of our faculty. We worry about things like cooperative learning, calculus reform, and the use of computers in the classroom. People who are thinking about education in math in this department are thinking about those things. But WAC was certainly what got us thinking about educational issues.

A variant of this theme is a UC faculty member who embraced as an old friend the WAC idea that, early in the process, learners need to be encouraged to express themselves freely. But he applied this notion almost entirely in the area of graphics, not writing, and he probably would have done so even without the WAC workshop, since this philosophy was well formulated before he attended. He has, however, continued to develop his "just let it flow, get it down" teaching methods in the graphics medium, in the face of skepticism from some of his departmental colleagues.

2. WAC on Hold

A second theme that occurs in faculty stories is the sense that some of the things faculty want to do are on hold, usually because of external circumstances—a child is born, the person becomes department head, illness intervenes.

Faculty had the sense that they could and would come back to the issues and try the strategies again at some future time when external constraints were lifted. One example is a faculty member who, after the workshop, became embroiled as head of his troubled department.

His interview reflected his sense of weariness and embattlement. At that time, his memory of the workshop was functioning as a kind of touchstone, a vision of the peaceful kingdom, held in his mind's eye, when turmoil in his department and college had made the society around him seem anything but peaceful. "It showed me there are still good people at UC," said another faculty member in a similar situation.

3. Embracing, Then Winnowing

A third theme in some stories is the faculty member showing initial enthusiasm and adopting many WAC ideas, then becoming overwhelmed by the workload, and refining and winnowing WAC strategies.

In some stories, this pattern of enthusiasm and winnowing becomes recursive. The faculty member realizes that each new teaching direction raises its own problems and that a teaching journey is composed of reiterated cycles. A TSU health sciences faculty member, for example, found that her initial enthusiastic embrace of WAC ideas and her subsequent paperload problems spurred her on to a new stage in her journey.

> *"I used to have my students write every day, but when the class grew to fifty people, it was simply too much to cope with."*
>
> —UC

In another professional preparation course, "Introduction to the Health Professions," I had students write responses to guest speakers, . . . their career goals, and reflections about their peer presentations. In all, I looked through and graded about twenty-five students' workbooks, each with more than forty pages, and critiqued the work. After three semesters of this, I was so delighted with their learning, but so frustrated with my workload, that I decided to investigate how to grade smarter. It became the topic for my 1988 sabbatical.

> *"I haven't made the writer's group at all since my wife has been back teaching, and I've had to be home for the kids. So I'm out of the loop on that one."*
>
> —TSU

4. Little by Little

"WAC on hold" could, in the long run, blend into this next pattern, which we call "little by little." What distinguishes it from WAC on hold is the sense, on the faculty member's part, that she or he was making progress—slowly but surely. Sometimes the unevenness of progress was caused by external circumstances. Sometimes the limiting factors were personal working styles. Several faculty, especially those from Walvoord's workshops at Whitworth, which emphasized extensive preliminary work to make an assignment effective, talked about their habits of "procrastination" or their serendipitous course-planning strategies as a barrier to the kind of prior planning they knew such assignments required. As one faculty member said candidly:

> To be honest . . . I tend to procrastinate. And those ideas [about preparing effective assignments and stating explicit criteria for grading, as discussed in the workshop] require that you don't procrastinate, but that you front-load your efforts. . . . When I have gotten around to doing it, I have been very glad and gotten all kinds of positive reinforcement. And when I haven't gotten around to doing it, I feel like, "Oh, Help!" I mean, what am I going to do with this? . . . I think I'm making a little progress in terms of being deliberate about what I want to know from students, what I want to be able to see into their minds about, what I want them to learn—as opposed to, "How can I think of a thirty-point assignment that is good at this point in the term?"

5. The Road to Damascus

Some faculty members reflected the sense that WAC had been a significant turnaround for them. The sociologist whose multiple connections we explored on pages 68–71 (this volume) sees his transformation in this way:

> I guess at first [when I went to the workshop] I was looking for some way to get away from the teaching style I had, which was pretty much a little bit of lecture and then large-group discussion. I was really frustrated with it. I just didn't feel that the students were getting the sociological perspective that way. Some did, but some didn't. And I was kind of flailing about trying to figure out how I could get their lives connected up with sociology. Now [after the workshop] I use a whole series of worksheets in all my courses. [He explains how the worksheets encourage the students to think critically and to

connect their lives to sociology. See pages 69–70, this volume.] I think the sociological perspective was always there for the better students, the ones who really clicked into sociology— the natural sociologists. I enjoy those students. But I enjoy far more the student who comes in and thinks, "What a jerky class. What a lark this is." Those are the students I love to deal with. If I can just make them turn on to sociology, it's amazing to watch. Before the workshop, I felt that my course wasn't doing that well. I think it is now. I won't ever return to that old path.

6. New Worlds

WAC had taken some faculty into realms they had not dared to enter before. The common thread in their stories was the sense that WAC had spurred them to reach out. Several TSU faculty had been involved in WAC for fifteen to eighteen years, and we had data about them across all those years. Here we present the accounts of two of those faculty members for whom WAC was a spur to "new worlds."

Logarithmic Growth
—Virginia Johnson Anderson, Biology, TSU

Easily distracted by rustling palm trees, darting geckos, and beautiful island children drawn to laptop computers as moths to flames, I drafted my faculty story on a hotel patio in Tonga, an island paradise in the South Pacific. I splashed in turquoise-blue waters, saw black coral, ate sea cucumbers, photographed bat sanctuaries, frolicked with sea stars in offshore tide pools, and even danced the "Electric Slide" for the Queen of Tonga.

Yet, my most vivid Tongan memory is of eighteen U.S. Peace Corps volunteers engaged in a think-pair-share activity with their host country counterparts in what, to the best of anyone's knowledge, was the first writing-across-the-curriculum workshop in the Kingdom of Tonga. After the WAC conference, the eleven science teachers, seven TESLs (Teachers of English as a Second Language), fifteen Tongan primary and secondary teachers, three Tongan principals, and three Peace Corps staff members enjoyed a barbecue beside the lagoon. As I watched them talking in the sunset, I could not help but wonder if any of their lives would be as profoundly changed by WAC as mine has been.

In 1981, I was teaching biology at Towson State University in Maryland. I was over forty, had ten-plus years of teaching experience, an assistant professorship, and best of all, tenure. I was known as a good teacher and committee member. I got along well with all my colleagues, even the most difficult ones, because I wasn't a threat to anyone's success. Like almost one-third (eight out of twenty-four) TSU biology faculty members, I did not have the doctorate, though I did have some coursework toward it. Just three years earlier, the university provost had stated publicly for the first time that no one would be promoted in any rank without "an earned doctorate."

Maybe I was a second-class academic, but I was a first-class mom! I was the stereotypical, devoted, single parent who served cookies and conversation to my two preteens after school, let the kids make bike trails in my front yard, and welcomed anyone for dinner who didn't say "yuk." I was not only a doting parent, I was a dating one, too. Slowly, in the course of three years, my Wednesday night commute to graduate school fifty miles away had been rewarded, then replaced, by romantic dinners and plans.

I would love to tell you that it was great insight on my part or great recruitment by the WAC movement that led me to the 1981–1982 Baltimore Area Consortium for Writing Across the Curriculum (BACWAC) Institute for College Teachers, but it wasn't. I was thrilled-to-death pregnant! As fall classes started, I was looking for anything that offered released time, and the BACWAC project did that.

Barbara Walvoord, one of the BACWAC leaders, called to verify that I would be at the two-day kickoff retreat and offered to drive. Our conversation on the thirty-five-mile trip was exceptional. At the retreat itself, much of what the leaders were saying about writing being contextual seemed to make good sense, but I didn't have a clue as to what their references to "genre" meant. We talked in small groups about several readings that were mailed out, but of course, I hadn't read them. We worked in broad discipline groups on the first evening, but it was hard to relate anything to biology. Barbara's focus session on the differences between successful and unsuccessful writers was excellent, but then another presenter read his paper to us word for word.

However, the context of the WAC retreat was "A+." The leaders and participants were congenial; the food was excellent. I met people from my own university, like Fil Dowling, coordinator of the TSU advanced writing courses, and also people from other institutions. I left the two-day retreat looking forward to the next sessions.

We met again at Loyola College two weeks later, for a two-hour session—the first of eight. We all became active participants. One thing we did was to share our own writing in small groups. I never felt comfortable or rewarded in that activity, but others thought it was great. For me, the real excitement began when we started to discuss writing-to-learn activities. I loved adapting WAC ideas to biology! I felt like an educational craftsperson, an inventor. I asked students to keep journals of their learning, had them write practice final exam questions, invited them to react freely to viewing human fetuses in lab, had them interview one another about their progress on an assignment, stopped a lecture and had everyone write for five minutes contrasting today's phylum with the previous Wednesday's. With all this new focus, the biology topics on which I had routinely lectured for ten years—prokaryotic cells, arthropods, glycolysis, DNA, RNA, ATP, mitosis, meiosis, dicotyledons—suddenly came to life again,

Speaking of life, my darling son Billy was born on February 4, 1982. He was bundled off to WAC workshops in March and April. I delivered the last ten "General Biology" lectures of the term with Billy sleeping, almost unnoticed, in a Snuggly™ on my back. That summer, Randy (15), Sherry (12), plus Cheney (16) and Jay (14), my "escalator children" (our family made up the phrase because they were much too wonderful to be called stepchildren), plus the baby and I spent most of our time at the swim club. While the older children swam and Billy slept peacefully under the umbrella, I began working on my dissertation . . . again (year nine at the University of Maryland).

This time, things were different. WAC had raised my self-esteem as a writer and researcher. Investigating the effect of kinetic structure and micrograph content on the ability of college biology students to read micrographs became a task, not a nemesis. Although I was busy getting a doctoral committee set up, compiling scanned electron micrographs, collecting research data, and teaching, I did not want to let go of my WAC support system. So I agreed to work on projects with Fil Dowling and Barbara Walvoord.

As the coordinator of the TSU advanced writing courses, Fil observed several of the discipline-based advanced writing courses in the fall of 1982. He selected my Biology 381, "Biological Literature."

I loved having Fil visit! I got all the joys of colleague collaboration that we had had in WAC, and I didn't even have to park at Loyola College. Support came to me. Fil brought handouts, readings, checklists, enthusiasm, questioning, and good research-based suggestions. He bolstered my confidence in grading; he gave me a great handout suggesting that teachers grade content first, organization second, and style third. He was a tremendous help in getting me to select a meaningful variety of writing assignments—he saved me from the term paper! By the end of that semester, the course assignments were well defined.

Before WAC, I told myself that students wrote poorly in their biology courses because they didn't spend enough time doing it and/or they had not been adequately trained in English 101. Disabused of those myths, I wanted to know more about how and why students had difficulty writing in "Bio Lit." Over coffee in October, Barbara and I decided to collaborate. We would examine how my upper-level biology students conducted and composed their original scientific research reports.

Little did we know that we had taken the first step in an eight-year journey. And a slow step at that. Having collected data from my class in 1983, we never even took the data out of the box until June 1984. No wonder—in the intervening year, I had finished my dissertation, ended my short but wonderfully "reproductive" marriage, defended my thesis, and received my doctorate. By July, we were listening to tapes, reading drafts, studying writers' logs, and figuring out how my students conducted and composed original science research. The fascinating things we learned led to two more years of data collection. Our collaboration became part of a "research merger"; it was integrated into a larger study with Walvoord and other WAC colleagues: Lucille McCarthy, John Breihan, Kim Sherman, and Sue Robison (1991).

As a biologist, I have spent many hours culturing one-celled protozoa. These fascinating life forms have three important stages in early development: inoculation, incubation, and logarithmic (log) growth. Since 1985, my professional life has been in the log-growth stage. Barbara invited me to do a small science part in several local presentations. Wow! I loved sharing my enthusiasm and techniques for writing-to-learn in science. The next thing I knew, she invited me to southern Maryland and then Pennsylvania. Within a year, I was doing WAC workshops on my own. To date, I have given nearly 100 WAC workshops at colleges, universities, and K–12 schools in the United States, Canada, and the Kingdom of Tonga. Barbara and I have co-authored papers for more than twenty national, regional, and local conferences in biology and composition.

I really believe that I learned to be a successful writer in WAC. I had not really understood the components of good writing. Now, I realize the strategic importance of identifying the audience in writing academic, scientific, and particularly grant-oriented prose. Since 1985, I've written three book chapters or sections, two juried journal articles, five faculty development grants, two faculty research grants, and five externally funded grants.

To me, faculty development is the sum total of all the processes that induce and/or enable faculty to "grow into" rather than "give up on" truly successful and satisfying academic careers. For all those who are concerned with faculty development—colleagues, department chairs, deans, provosts, presidents, and chancellors—here are some suggestions:

1. Offer all kinds of incentives—money, time, scheduling help—for faculty to try WAC and/or other promising faculty development projects because it doesn't matter *why* people sign up to grow, just that they do. My motives were definitely self-serving, but look what happened.

2. Construct faculty development programs that meet more than once. Get them to commit to an opening session and then several more sessions later. Often, new ideas take a while to click. I wasn't turned on to WAC ideas until I tried them in my class.

3. Design faculty development programs that can combat professional isolation. Teachers like myself, who are juggling family responsibilities or graduate work, become more and more isolated from professional thinking. We're not socially isolated—I drank coffee with the gang in the biology lounge and had a Halloween party in my prep room—but we are professionally isolated. We may or may not go to good seminars, but we never have time to stay and talk to the speakers. We don't network; we just work.

4. Insist on diversity. TSU's summer workshops had elementary, secondary, and university teachers solving problems together. Faculty who are just getting by need to see successful faculty up close. I was amazed in those early WAC meetings when one Ph.D. full professor praised my teaching technique; I'd never shared one with a professor.

5. Capitalize on different academic disciplinary viewpoints. WAC is successful because its whole is much greater than its parts. I vividly remember listening with Barbara to my students' think-aloud tapes and hearing biology students struggle for hours to write the introductions to their research reports. I said to Barbara, "Why would they try to write the introduction before they had ever done any research? I can't understand it?" She explained very matter-of-factly, "Students often mistake the order of format for the order of composition." Now that would have taken me several years of biology reports to figure out.

6. Recognize that WAC and other forms of innovative faculty development work far more effectively and holistically than are ever documented. WAC projects often measure their success only by how writing programs and/or skills have changed within a discipline. That is a conservative measure of WAC success. WAC gave me the teaching tools and leadership skills to develop several excellent classroom activities, workshops, and community programs related to TSU's Mainstreaming Women's Studies three-year FIPSE grant (another case illustrating that it doesn't matter *why* you go, but *that* you go to faculty development programs. The chair just said, "Do it").

As a result of rave reviews of a WAC workshop, I was asked by the head of the Office of Science of the Maryland State Department of Education to sponsor a funded workshop on hands-on science and writing for elementary teachers. That workshop precipitated a meeting in which I was asked to head up a new pilot elementary science in-service project. It became the prototype for the Urban Science Teaching Project, which was recently funded by the National Science Foundation. Since 1986, I have brought in more than $400,000 in external grants to TSU.

In closing, my personal life is in log phase, too. I married Cliff and *finally* know what a happy marriage is. Randy is an appraiser and makes almost as much money as I do. Sherry is in graduate school, and darling Billy is in the seventh grade. Out of the eight of us who did not have doctorates in 1981, I am the only one who got a degree. Some have retired; most have been inundated with departmental work. All are still good teachers, but their salaries and their self-esteem suffer. Thank you, mentors, and thank you writing-across-the-curriculum colleagues—I doubt whether I would have made it without you.

Transforming a Career

—H. Fil Dowling Jr., English, TSU

Can a hardworking, gently introverted, limelight-shunning English professor undergo a major career transformation as a result of the writing-across-the-curriculum (WAC) movement?

You bet. I know, because it happened to me!

Back in the spring of 1981, I had been at Towson State University (TSU) for fifteen years. I was a teacher, pure and simple. I had never aspired to be a scholar, and TSU prior to the 1980s had shown little interest in my becoming one. Originally a state teachers' college, TSU had always been dedicated to good undergraduate teaching. And that's what I was—a consistently good teacher, according to both student and peer evaluations. But though my reputation as an effective teacher and committee chair was known and respected within my department, I was virtually unknown to the campus at large. In fact, one of my colleagues, writing a promotion recommendation for me in the early 1980s, referred to me as "the best-kept secret in the English department."

What happened to change this situation? I was a tree that needed to grow more roots. The root influences I needed began to come in 1981, in the form of new approaches to teaching writing, with their firm commitment to writing in all disciplines. This root nourishment that I received not only revitalized my career but also enabled me to put out branches, in the form of WAC workshops and other activities, to other faculty at Towson. These branches in turn sprouted seeds—co-workers who developed into trees of their own, conveying WAC ideas to still more faculty. Roots, trees, branches, seeds, and new trees—these are the metaphors of my development as a TSU faculty member since 1981.

In terms of roots, chief among my exposures to WAC were the Baltimore Area Consortium for Writing Across the Curriculum (BACWAC) and the Maryland Writing Project. BACWAC is a unique group, founded by Barbara Walvoord and others, which brings together Baltimore-area teachers from all disciplines and from kindergarten through college for faculty development activities. The Maryland Writing Project was originally developed through BACWAC's sponsorship, and then it later absorbed BACWAC as one of its parts.

Having a sabbatical during 1981–1982 motivated me to enroll in the first annual Maryland Writing Project Summer Institute in July 1981, co-led by Barbara Walvoord, who became an important influence. At this institute, for the first time in my career, I was surrounded by teachers from elementary school through college, some of them not English teachers. For the first time, I read avidly in composition theory and in the practice of composition instruction, becoming acquainted with Britton, Emig, Murray, Flower, Sommers, Maimon, and other pioneers of the new rhetoric. For the first time,

I stood in front of a group of my peers to give a seventy-five-minute presentation on teaching writing. And for the first time, I became a member of a peer writing group—joining with three other Summer Institute participants, chosen at random, who hesitantly, and then with increasing confidence, shared pieces of our personal and professional writing with each other. Then, too, as I shared social occasions with these new colleagues at the Summer Institute, I found that despite being shy, I enjoyed their company and was stimulated by their thoughts about teaching and about life.

The following spring of 1982, I co-led a BACWAC workshop on teaching writing for college faculty in all disciplines, put together by Barbara Walvoord and two of her colleagues at Loyola College in Maryland.

I soon became involved in a number of BACWAC-run activities, and eventually became coordinator of BACWAC in the late 1980s. Also in 1982, I volunteered for and was chosen to assume a newly created position at Towson, coordinator of the Advanced Writing Course Program, our WAC program. An additional root influence was a 1984 two-week seminar I attended at Georgetown University entitled "Approaches to Teaching Writing." This seminar's leader, James Slevin, added to my insight into the WAC movement by introducing me to its more radical side: its potential to *transform* as well as improve the writing, and thinking, of faculty and students from various disciplines.

In what ways was the "tree" of my faculty career affected by its strengthened root system? I can think of at least ten (Figure 8.1 summarizes them), not all of which I need to describe here; but several do deserve details.

The main change in my teaching of writing, besides the fact that I began to use such now well-known and widely used approaches as "the writing process" and "peer-response groups," involved adapting the WAC concept of "writing-to-learn" to my literature classes. Abandoning the hoary but often futile "term paper," I developed instead a system centered on nongraded journal writing and classroom projects that focused on helping students develop key skills they needed to become more effective and responsive readers of literature. The sample classroom exercise included here (Figure 8.2) illustrates the methods I've developed. I use this exercise early in the semester to introduce students to the concepts of *observing* and *interpreting* literature. Through exercises such as this, students, including non-English majors, are intrigued to discover that they can make a number of significant observations about a piece of literature that they don't fully understand, which they can then use as the basis for better *interpretations* of the work than they believed themselves capable of.

All of my altered teaching methods resulted in less lecturing and more interaction between my students and me, and among themselves. In short, as a result of my WAC roots, the part of my career that involved teaching (which at one time had been the whole of my career) became more innovative, more exciting to me, and more genuinely helpful to students.

Main Exposure to WAC Theory and Practice

The Baltimore Area Consortium for Writing Across the Curriculum

The Maryland Writing Project (a branch of the National Writing Project)

Seminar in "Approaches to Teaching Writing" at Georgetown University

Results of Exposure to WAC

Coordinator of Towson State University's WAC Program, 1982–present

Chair of multidisciplinary committee that guides Towson State's Advanced Writing Course Program, 1977–present

Coordinator of the Baltimore Area Consortium for Writing Across the Curriculum, 1987–1990; Steering Committee, 1985–1993

Co-director of Institute on Teaching Writing Across the Curriculum for Baltimore-area college faculty, Spring 1982

Coordinator and Co-leader of two-day workshops for Towson State faculty on teaching WAC, 1984–present

Author of publications and conference papers on WAC and related subjects

Contributions of WAC to My Faculty Career

Changed methods of teaching writing

Changed use of writing in subject-discipline courses (literature)

Improved teaching (Towson State has mandatory student evaluation of teaching)

Improved assertiveness

Improved leadership ability

Improved public-speaking confidence

Improved visibility, on and off campus

Developed a body of publications, conference presentations, and workshops

Contributed significantly to "promotability"

Enabled other faculty at Towson State to develop *their* careers further through exposure to WAC

Figure 8.1. Summary of Fil Dowling's WAC-related career development.

Equally important to my career development were "intangible" effects of my exposure to WAC, such as increased assertiveness, leadership, and speaking confidence. In the fall of 1981, energized by the recent Maryland Writing Project Summer Institute and realizing the effective role I had played in it, I gathered the courage to ask Barbara Walvoord, out of the blue, if I could join as a co-leader the WAC workshop she was planning with two of her Loyola

---

Excerpt from a Story for Observations

[The following passage is from William Dean Howells's short story entitled "Editha." In this story, Editha and George are engaged. Editha, strong-willed and patriotic, has insisted that George, a pacifist, volunteer as a soldier in the Civil War, against his better judgment. In the passage below, Editha and George are saying goodbye before George leaves for the war.]

They strained each other in embraces that seemed as ineffective as their words, and he kissed her face with quick, hot breaths that were so unlike him, that made her feel as if she had lost her old lover and found a stranger in his place. The stranger said: "What a gorgeous flower you are, with your red hair, and your blue eyes that look black now, and your face with the color painted out by the white moonshine! Let me hold you under the chin, to see whether I love blood, you tiger-lily!" Then he laughed Gearson's laugh and released her, scared and giddy. Within her wilfulness she had been frightened by a sense of subtler force in him, and mystically mastered as she had never been before.

1. What *observations* can you make about the passage above? (Observations are a reading skill. When we read anything, we make observations about things in the work we are reading that help us *understand* what the work is saying. We also make observations about things in the work that we think are important in some way, even though we may not be sure exactly how or why they are important.)

2. After making observations about the passage, can you interpret what it implies to the reader about Editha and about George? (By *analyzing* the observations we make about something that we read, we can arrive at a fuller interpretation of their significance. To analyze, we examine in depth the individual observations we have made; how they relate to each other; and how they relate to the whole story or poem they come from [i.e., how they relate to the context].)

Figure 8.2. Fil Dowling's journal assignment.

College colleagues in the spring of 1982. When Barbara graciously consented, the future direction of my career suddenly became clear: I was to become (among other things) a WAC specialist. Although this 1982 workshop was just moderately successful, as only Barbara, among the four of us, had ever led a workshop before, it was a tremendous learning experience and gave me the confidence that I could organize and run WAC workshops of my own.

I was now ready to take on leadership roles that I had shied away from before. I generated ideas for, organized, and co-led a number of faculty development workshops in WAC at Towson State. (Almost all of the TSU faculty who contributed narratives and interviews for this book either attended or co-led, or both, one or more of those workshops.) I visited the classes of willing TSU faculty for four-week periods, consulting with them on student writing and new techniques for teaching it. I started a faculty writing group at Towson. And by 1985, I was ready to assume some leadership roles off campus. I petitioned for and was accepted as head editor of the *Maryland English Journal* (an affiliate journal of NCTE), a position I held for five years. And in 1987, I put together and submitted my first proposal for a panel session—three papers by three different faculty—at the CCCC (Conference on College Composition and Communication). This became the first of a number of papers I have since given at CCCC, Penn State, and several other professional conferences.

It's worth noting that my proposing of panel groups for CCCC was a far cry from my earlier career backwardness when it came to public speaking— outside the safety of a classroom, that is. I'm amused to recall that when I gave my first sabbatical report in the late 1970s, before a small and admittedly *friendly* group of English department faculty, I begged my elderly parents to attend, for moral and, if necessary, even physical support! (The latter, fortunately, wasn't needed.) I faced each new type of public-speaking role as a distinct challenge. My first time leading a workshop at TSU, my first shakily delivered paper at CCCC, my first presentation at TSU's January Conference for Faculty, and my first time as solo conductor of an off-campus writing workshop (at a Canadian Council of Teachers of English conference in Vancouver in 1989) were all innovations in my career. But my WAC root influences had done their work well, and by the 1990s, I had become a veteran of public appearances.

Another result of my involvement in WAC was increased visibility. Before I became coordinator of Towson State's WAC program, I had little name recognition beyond the English department. But through my activities in that role, I met and interacted with a wealth of dynamic, interesting faculty. Just as one example, the Faculty Writers' Response Group I started for Towson State faculty in 1985 turned out to strengthen collegial ties and mutual respect just as much as it helped to strengthen faculty writing. Faculty in this writing group, as well as faculty in the WAC workshops I've given, frequently cite getting to know and interact with faculty in other departments as a major, positive result.

By this time my career tree had developed many branches—branches carrying WAC ideas and influences to my fellow faculty. Written evaluations by participants in the two-day WAC workshops I developed were highly enthusiastic and praiseworthy. Equally important, the workshops generated new leaders, new carriers of WAC ideas on campus. I promoted workshop participants to co-leaders of future workshops. I recruited them to serve on the Advanced Writing Course Subcommittee, which oversees the WAC course program at Towson State. I invited them to join my writing group for faculty, which not only encourages its members to generate and revise publishable writing, thus enhancing their careers, but also models WAC methods like peer-response groups, writing-to-learn, and the draft-and-revise process, which faculty can then import back into their own writing classrooms.

In short, as branches, various faculty development activities—sprung from the nourished tree of my career, they often developed seeds—interested and revitalized faculty, who then became flourishing trees of their own, in turn putting out branches to influence still other faculty on campus and beyond.

Of course, there were failures as well. I learned that no person and no set of ideas would have a positive effect on everybody. I recall the apathy from some members of my own English department that greeted my enthusiasm after I had taken the 1981 MWP institute. (Could "they"—K–12 teachers— really have anything to teach "us"?) And I remember vividly one of several faculty members outside of the English department who simply could not be reached. This person, whose department felt him to be unsuccessful at teaching writing, was enticed by them to enroll in the MWP institute in the mid-1980s, and at my urging he also attended several mini-workshops on WAC that I gave on school-day afternoons. Yet, when I made some invited visits to this faculty member's writing class, I discovered that all of the new writing-instruction ideas that the teacher had been exposed to, and did use, served merely as a thin overlay on the traditional writing teacher's attitude: "I tell you what to write; you write it; I tell you if it's any good or not."

I gradually realized that new trees would come only from faculty who were *self*-motivated: people who appropriated WAC ideas for their own purposes and in support of their own goals of faculty development. Many of these faculty have become "writing specialists" themselves, disseminating WAC ideas to other faculty in their own disciplines, at TSU at large, or through national workshops and conventions. Several of these people are the faculty whose stories you have read in this book. But there are others.

I think, for instance, of Linda Mahin, an English teacher who joined the Advanced Writing Course Subcommittee in the mid-1980s, co-led our first two-day WAC workshop in 1984, and then applied WAC ideas to her specialty area of business writing, becoming a recognized scholar and consultant in that field. I think of Linda Sweeting, in chemistry, whose first contact with WAC came when she joined the Faculty Writers' Response Group in 1990 because she wanted to make her own writing more facile and more appropriate to varied audiences. Although originally opposed to having a writing course in chemistry because "scientists can't teach writing," Linda has since created her own WAC course, called "Ethics in the Sciences," and also composed published pieces for both professional and general audiences. I think of Charlotte Exner, who, encouraged by the enthusiasm of her department chair about one of our two-day workshops, agreed to let me visit her writing course in occupational therapy, developed new teaching methods for it which she passed on to subsequent teachers of the course, and who, after she became department chair, encouraged several of her newer faculty to attend our later WAC workshops.

And I think of the entire nursing department at TSU (of all the unexpected departments to be strongly influenced by the winds of WAC!). After dutifully, though not eagerly, developing its own writing course in the late 1970s to meet TSU's new general education requirements, the nursing staff fretted over how the course was working out. They consequently sent faculty to our two-day WAC workshops—eleven faculty in all, more than any other department. In 1986, they invited Virginia Anderson, who by then had become a science writing specialist, to consult with them as a department. Later, they called in more advisors on teaching writing in the health professions, including Joan McMahon. And one member of the nursing faculty joined first the faculty writing group and later, at my invitation, the Advanced Writing Course Subcommittee. Ultimately, the nursing department thought so deeply about WAC ideas and the writing of their nursing majors that their thinking progressed *beyond* Towson's requirements for a writing course. They are currently developing an innovative plan to sequence various levels of student writing experiences throughout their undergraduate program, instead of relying on a single, senior-level course to "fix the students' writing."

To conclude, two important results of WAC's influence on my faculty career are that it helped me become "promotable" and that it enabled me to make contributions to *other* faculty's career development. Briefly, about promotability: by the mid-1980s, when it became necessary at TSU for faculty up for promotion to have a significant record of scholarly productivity and publication, I had developed enough publications and papers, most of them centered on WAC, to meet that standard, and I was promoted to full professor in 1988. (Interestingly, these scholarly activities had no negative effects on my teaching performance; in fact, my student evaluations, which had always been good, became still higher throughout the 1980s and 1990s.) It wasn't only the scholarly production that made me promotable, but also the fact that my name was by then well known and respected around campus because of all the WAC-related activities I had sponsored. I was no longer "the best-kept secret in the English department."

However, even more important than the promotability, I'm most happy about the enabling role I've been able to play in the development of *other* faculty careers at Towson State. One faculty member's career development is important; but more important is the entire "life" of a university—its collective faculty. The impact of WAC on my faculty career firmly illustrates that WAC can be and has been a *major* influence on college faculty development in general. We at Towson State are the living, ever-growing, still-changing proof.

9 Conclusions and Implications

Summary of Findings

Our study affirms previous research which suggests that WAC influences teachers, often in significant ways. But we have operated not in the match-to-sample or "resistance" frameworks common to much previous research: we have tried not to define what *we* think WAC is but to let those definitions emerge from the faculty. We have viewed faculty not as adopters or resisters but, in the words of Hargreaves (1988), as "creators of meaning, interpreters of the world and all it asks of them . . . people striving for purpose and meaning in circumstances that are usually much less than ideal and which call for constant adjustment, adaptation, and redefinition." We have tried to ask, therefore, in Hargreaves's words, "how teachers manage to cope with, adapt to, and reconstruct their circumstances . . . what they achieve, not what they fail to achieve" (216).

We found that faculty often came to WAC to work on problems and goals they had already articulated or because they believe in periodic reflection and renewal. Their image of themselves as self-directed managers of their own growth underlies the entire study. Faculty often remembered WAC events—workshops, faculty response groups—in terms of community. For many, the WAC community was characterized by safety, liberation, the sort of naming that gave them language for what they were doing, support for their own growth, and validation of the importance of teaching. But a few remembered a "true believer" mentality or a top-down presentational mode that compromised community.

At UC, 99 percent of a faculty sample reported changing their teaching in some way as a result of their WAC workshop. When faculty identified the most important things they had learned from WAC, they often described not particular strategies but changes in their philosophies and attitudes about teaching. They altered their theories about teaching and learning, acquired new habits of mind, found new confidence and enthusiasm, and changed their own roles in relation to their students.

WAC also changed particular teaching strategies. Faculty were often quite explicit about the impact of WAC on their strategies, but some were not always sure whether to classify a strategy as "WAC." At times, their definitions of "WAC" differed. Faculty tended to concentrate not on adopting or resisting WAC per se but on finding what strategies "worked" for their particular settings. The same criteria were used to decide that a WAC strategy had "worked" as to decide that it had not "worked." The criteria concerned whether the strategy had helped create community in the classroom, whether it enhanced student learning, whether it was feasible, and whether it fit the teacher's own personal priorities and teaching style. Teaching strategies tended to shift and change over time to some extent, regardless of whether they were perceived to "work"; faculty reported themselves as constantly changing, as constantly experimenting with their teaching.

WAC affected career patterns as well as teaching. Patterns were complex and intermingled, and influences were often impossible to isolate. However, we noted six themes:

- "The Road Not Taken," in which faculty were active in educational reform but in a way they saw as not directly connected to WAC;

- "WAC on Hold," where a new baby or a new department chairship meant that they did not have time or attention to push WAC forward;

- "Embracing, Then Winnowing," in which they tried to implement many things from WAC, became overwhelmed, and then had to select what they could do;

- "Little by Little," in which they saw themselves as making slow, uneven progress;

- "The Road to Damascus," where there was a revolutionary turnaround in their thinking or teaching; and, finally,

- "New Worlds," in which WAC served as a spur to move outward in many directions which faculty had previously not imagined for themselves.

These conclusions are drawn from data collected throughout periods of years at each institution. Until 1993–1994, data were collected without any knowledge that they would one day be combined into a single study. In 1993–1995, a series of forty-two interviews and faculty-authored accounts on all three campuses addressed a comparable set of questions. These lent some consistency to the data and served as the culmination to the stories of faculty on whom we had collected other data over the years. They also gave us many of the direct quotations from faculty that fill this book.

The body of data for this study, as a whole, is characterized by its variety and wealth. The largest part of it is the faculty self-reports, which we viewed as strong data because they revealed faculty perceptions and because the point of the study was to see WAC through faculty eyes. But we are also aware that if one's goal is to find out what changes actually occurred in an empirical sense, self-reports are relatively weak data. Our self-reports, then, are supported in many cases by syllabi, other course documents, classroom observations, observations of teachers at work on committees and in discussion groups, and student interviews and questionnaires.

We are also aware that the "testimonial" genre still influences our report. It seemed inevitable that in the interviews, sponsored by the WAC office, teachers would try to cooperate by telling what WAC had done for them. We tried to avoid this syndrome by having the interviews conducted by someone other than the workshop director, by using data where the faculty member had spoken in a group or for some other purpose, and so on, as we detailed in the methods chapter. But we acknowledge that the influence of WAC may have been forefronted for our faculty, simply by the fact of our asking.

Nonetheless, the themes we describe here were strong and clear in the data throughout the years and in all types of data.

Implications for WAC Programs

What did we, as WAC directors, learn from our own study?

1. We learned not to imagine that faculty came to WAC in a vacuum. They had, we discovered, already articulated plans, philosophies, and agendas. We realized that WAC leaders need to know what those are and to help faculty to build upon them.

2. We learned that faculty will end up defining WAC differently, or ambiguously, and that it doesn't matter. The important thing, we concluded, was for them to shape a definition that is meaningful to them. In fact, the definition of WAC was not nearly as important as the definition of "what works." *That*, we believe, is the definition that faculty developers need to focus on because it's the definition that drives a faculty member's decision to adopt or drop a particular teaching strategy.

3. We learned that the richest gift we could offer to faculty were resources for their own development. We learned not to try completely to predict or control that development, but to suggest, from our own knowledge, how it might go, and then to leave the faculty mem-

ber to integrate our knowledge with his or her own. We learned to trust that synthesis. Our role, we learned, was to stimulate, not to evangelize.

4. The atmosphere, the kind of community, that is created at WAC events will be long remembered and is crucial to the impact of WAC on faculty. Faculty will seek in WAC and in their own classrooms those elements that help them to achieve community. We believe that WAC directors cannot give too much emphasis to the nature of the communities they form and facilitate.

5. The faculty will perhaps be helped more by the philosophies and attitudes they take away than by specific strategies. WAC directors might then work to make their philosophies clear and visible and to help faculty do the same. But not in the abstract—through concrete example, through lived experience.

6. We learned that perhaps the most valuable contribution WAC can make to a faculty member is to be a source of renewed commitment and enthusiasm.

7. We learned the imperative of building our programs not as one-shot workshops, not as camp-meeting conversions, but as a network of ongoing support for career-long development. Faculty, we saw, benefited from support, community, and constant stimulation, across time. To do that, WAC needs to collaborate with other faculty development efforts. WAC, we believe, must see itself as part of a network of different kinds of programs that together can serve needs for growth and community (see Walvoord 1996).

Perhaps the final outcomes for us as WAC directors on our own campuses were humility, trust, and awe:

- humility that we cannot win converts to our vision, nor be so arrogant as to imagine that faculty are even focused on accepting or rejecting WAC. They're not—they're focused on finding what works for them;
- trust that those same faculty have the resources and the intelligence to engineer their own career-long development;
- awe at the complex, creative, sometimes crazy, always fascinating directions that development can take. Awe at what emerges when we focus, in Hargreaves's words, not on what faculty fail to do but on what they achieve—in the long run.

Appendix A

University of Cincinnati Questionnaire on Teaching Changes, Administered to a Random Sample of Faculty, 1993–1994

QUESTIONNAIRE

INSTRUCTIONS: Please read each question carefully and *circle* the number of the response that *best* represents your opinion.

General Information

1.   What is your present position? (circle your answer)

    1.   Full-time faculty

    2.   Part-time faculty

    3.   Administrator with a teaching responsibility

    4.   Administrator with no teaching responsibility

2.   What is your tenure status?

    1.   Tenured

    2.   Tenure track but not yet tenured

    3.   Not on tenure track

Changes in Undergraduate Teaching

3.   In the past twelve months, have you taught at least one course that included at least some undergraduates? (circle your answer)

    Yes   No

    If you marked "no," please skip to the instructions on the last page.

The following questions ask about *change* in your undergraduate teaching. They are *not* an evaluation of the quality of your teaching.

4.   In the past twelve months, I have made a change in my undergraduate teaching which I believe has resulted in enhanced student learning. (circle your answer)

    Yes   No

    If you marked "no," please skip to question 7.

Types of Changes

5. The following are some types of teaching changes that the research suggests might improve undergraduate student learning. However, you may have decided against any of these changes because you are already doing these things, because you believe they would not enhance student learning, or because they would be impractical, given your teaching load, class size, etc. Further, "improvement" is highly dependent on classroom context, and you may have taken other actions that improved your students' learning. Thus, again, we are not judging the quality of your teaching but recording types of changes. Please circle the letters in front of all changes you have made in the past twelve months. If you have made no changes, please go to question 7.

    a. Increased the amount of written/oral/visual/musical/clinical or similar work I require from my undergraduate students.

    b. Increased in-class discussion and interaction with my undergraduate students.

    c. Increased student collaboration and/or peer review in an undergraduate class.

    d. Provided more frequent and/or fuller feedback to my undergraduate students on their progress.

    e. Stated course goals or objectives more explicitly in my syllabus or handouts.

    f. Stated criteria for grading more explicitly in my syllabus or handouts.

    g. Increased my guidance of students as they are working on their assignments.

    h. Changed my way of questioning or interacting with students so as to encourage deeper thinking.

    i   Increased my interaction with my undergraduate students outside of class.

    j. Focused less on what *I cover* and more on what *students learn.*

    k. Other (please describe).

Factors that Influenced Changes in Your Undergraduate Teaching

6. *If* in the past twelve months you made changes designed to enhance undergraduate student learning, how influential were the factors below in helping or motivating you to change? (circle your answer)

FACTORS HELPING/MOTIVATING ME TO CHANGE MY UNDERGRADUATE TEACHING DURING THE PAST TWELVE MONTHS

		Extremely Influential	Very Influential	Somewhat Influential	Slightly Influential	Not at all Influential
a.	My own satisfaction.	5	4	3	2	1
b.	Wanted to improve student work.	5	4	3	2	1
c.	Feedback from students.	5	4	3	2	1
d.	Feedback from colleague(s).	5	4	3	2	1
e.	Feedback from department head or similar administrator(s).	5	4	3	2	1
f.	Feedback from TA(s).	5	4	3	2	1
g.	Perceived that teaching was becoming more important in my department or similar unit.	5	4	3	2	1
h.	Perceived that teaching was becoming more important and valued in my college.	5	4	3	2	1
i.	Perceived that teaching was becoming more important at UC in general.	5	4	3	2	1
j.	Needed to improve my teaching for upcoming reappointment, promotion, or tenure review.	5	4	3	2	1
k.	Workshop or conference sponsored by UC.	5	4	3	2	1
l.	Workshop or conference *not* sponsored by UC.	5	4	3	2	1
m.	I wanted to try for a teaching award.	5	4	3	2	1
n.	I had more time to work on my teaching.	5	4	3	2	1
o.	My personal priorities are moving more toward teaching.	5	4	3	2	1
p.	Additional resources made changes possible (e.g., new equipment, staff).	5	4	3	2	1
q.	New configuration of class time.	5	4	3	2	1
r.	Externally mandated changes in course content or methods (e.g., department, accrediting agency).	5	4	3	2	1

s.	I changed or more clearly articulated my goals for the course.	5	4	3	2	1
t.	New course prompted change.	5	4	3	2	1
u.	My department/school/college's participation in the Project to Improve and Reward Teaching (PIRT).	5	4	3	2	1
v.	Offering an honors course.	5	4	3	2	1
w.	Availability of a new textbook/edition.	5	4	3	2	1
x.	Reading about teaching.	5	4	3	2	1
y.	Visiting someone else's class.	5	4	3	2	1
z.	New technological advances (e.g., new computer software, networking capability, lab equipment, etc.).	5	4	3	2	1
aa.	New advances in my field.	5	4	3	2	1
bb.	Other (please describe).					

_____

_____   5   4   3   2   1

7. What are the one or two most important things that UC could do to make it easier for you to change your undergraduate teaching in ways you think would be conducive to better undergraduate student learning?

_____

_____

_____

Appendix B

Whitworth College Questionnaire to Faculty Teaching W-I Courses, 1995

1995 SURVEY OF W-I COURSES AT WHITWORTH COLLEGE

Course Information

(Please complete the following table.)

Course title and number	
Average enrollment	
Maximum enrollment	
Average class standing (Soph, Jr, Sr)	
Are TAs used in teaching or grading?	
Would TAs be useful? (if not already in use)	
Is this a required or elective course in major?	
Is a departmental style sheet or handbook available to students?	

Required Writing Assignments

(Please complete the following table.)

	Writing assignment	Number of assignments	Page requirement	Are faculty-student conferences required? (Y/N)	Is peer editing done?	What documentation format is used? (APA, MLA, other)	Are students referred to Writing Center?	How important is grammar in evaluation? (% of grade)
In-class								
Formal essay								
Lab report								
Journal								
Other (specify)								
Other (specify)								

Resources for Teaching Writing-Intensive Courses

(Indicate which items you would find helpful. Additional comments are appreciated.)

Resources on writing in your discipline	
TAs for peer consulting and grading	
Consulting with other faculty	
Training workshops	
Peer review (e.g., faculty visits to class)	
Released time	
Internet consulting	

PLEASE ANSWER THE FOLLOWING QUESTIONS:

1. If conferences are required, how often are they done?

2. What are your policies and procedures regarding the revision, rewriting, and resubmission of writing assignments?

3. If writing instruction is given during class time, what topics are covered? (circle all that apply)

    style   documentation/notation   grammar   editing   rhetoric   organization

4. Are you interested in a colloquium focused on W-I-designated courses at Whitworth College? (circle your answer)

    Yes   No

5. What objectives, regarding writing competence, do you have for students in your major?

    How successful do you think W-I-designated courses have been in achieving these objectives?

6. If you have referred students to the Writing Center, have you encountered any problems? If yes, explain.

Additional comments:

Appendix C

University of Cincinnati Questionnaire to Faculty on WAC Outcomes, 1991–1992

[Note: the initial questions asked about demographic information.]

5. As a result of the Shakertown workshop, I have made at least some changes in my teaching.

    Yes   No

6. The changes I have made (mark all that apply):

    ___ Adding more or different writing assignments to the course.

    ___ Changing my existing writing assignments in some way (i.e., changing the wording of the assignment sheet, giving different kinds of instructions or guidance, changing grading practices or criteria, etc.).

    ___ Beginning to use, or changing my use of, peer collaboration/review.

    ___ Giving more guidance to students during the writing process.

    ___ Using writing to stimulate class discussion.

    ___ More conscious of my goals in developing assignments.

    ___ Taken some action within the department, college, university, or discipline to promote WAC.

    Please explain:

    _____

    _____

    ___ Made a presentation or published about WAC.

    Please give the full reference:

    _____

    _____

7. The best thing that happened as a result of WAC is:

    _____

    _____

    _____

8.   Problems or questions that have arisen are:

_____

_____

_____

9.   Final comments (use reverse side if needed):

_____

_____

_____

Appendix D

Whitworth College Questionnaire to Students in W-I Courses, 1989–1991

The Whitworth faculty have made a commitment to help students improve their writing. Because of this, many of our courses include a writing component. We would appreciate your comments on these efforts.

PLEASE CIRCLE:

strongly agree	agree	neutral	disagree	strongly disagree
1	2	3	4	5

The opportunity to rewrite papers was important to my progress as a writer:

1	2	3	4	5

Writing about the assigned topics helped me understand the course material:

1	2	3	4	5

The writing assignments proved challenging:

1	2	3	4	5

The assignments were expressed clearly:

1	2	3	4	5

- -

If you had a conference with a faculty member concerning a paper, in what ways did this prove helpful?

Which areas of your writing do you think improved this term (i.e., organizational structure, clarity of thinking and expression, use of supportive details, usage and grammar, etc.)?

In which areas of your writing do you most sense a need to improve?

Appendix E

Interview Questions Used on All Three Campuses, 1993–1995

[Note: These were semistructured interviews, so the interviewer did not necessarily ask the questions in order and felt free to follow up the interviewee's responses.]

1. What do you remember about your WAC experiences?

2. Why did you attend WAC?

3. What aspects of your experience in WAC seemed most important in impacting your teaching? In what ways?

4. How would you describe the types of changes you made?

5. As you look back over your history as a teacher since WAC, what would you identify as the sequence of changes you made? What changed first, second, third?

6. Is there one thing you did as a result of WAC that surprised you because it worked? Are there others?

7. Was there one thing that surprised you because it didn't work? How do you account for this?

8. What does the workshop mean to you now, as you look back?

9. What other teaching supports do you think you've taken advantage of as a result of your experience in WAC?

10. Can you describe peak moments in your teaching career?

11. [Interviewer collects any syllabi or class assignments and talks about them.]

Works Cited

Abbott, Michael M., Pearl W. Bartelt, Stephen M. Fishman, and Charlotte Honda. 1992. "Interchange: A Conversation among the Disciplines." In Herrington and Moran, 103–18.

Ackerman, John. 1993. "The Promise of Writing to Learn." *Written Communication* 10: 334–70.

Anderson, Virginia Johnson, and Barbara E. Walvoord. 1991. "Conducting and Reporting Original Scientific Research: Anderson's Biology Class." In Walvoord and McCarthy, 177–227.

Argyris, Chris. 1993. *Knowledge for Action: A Guide to Overcoming Barriers to Organizational Change.* San Francisco: Jossey-Bass.

Argyris, Chris, Robert Putnam, and Diana McLain Smith. 1985. *Action Science.* San Francisco: Jossey-Bass.

Astin, Helen S. 1993. "Responsive Faculty or Responding to Student Needs." In Weimer, 5–8.

Baldwin, Roger G. 1993. "The Evolving Career of the Vital College Teacher." In Weimer, 13–15.

Bean, Daniel J. 1992. "The World of Biology." In *A Community of Voices: Reading and Writing in the Disciplines,* edited by Toby Fulwiler and Arthur W. Biddle, 641–44. New York: Macmillan.

Beaver, John F., and Nancy Deal. 1990. "Writing Across the Entire Curriculum: A Status Report on Faculty Attitudes." Paper presented at the annual meeting of the Northeastern Educational Research Association. Ellenville, NY. October 31–November 2.

Belenky, Mary F., Blythe M. Clinchy, Nancy R. Goldberger, and Jill M. Tarule. 1986. *Women's Ways of Knowing: The Development of Self, Voice, and Mind.* New York: Basic Books.

Bishop, Wendy. 1990. *Something Old, Something New: College Writing Teachers and Classroom Change.* Carbondale: Southern Illinois University Press; Urbana, IL: Conference on College Composition and Communication/National Council of Teachers of English.

Braine, George. 1990. "Writing Across the Curriculum: A Case Study of Faculty Practices at a Research University." ERIC ED 324 680.

Bratcher, Suzanne, and Elizabeth J. Stroble. 1994. "Determining the Progression from Comfort to Confidence: A Longitudinal Evaluation of a National Writing Project Site Based on Multiple Data Sources." *Research in the Teaching of English* 28.1 (February): 66–88.

Carneson, John. 1994. "Investigating the Evolution of Classroom Practice." In Constable, Farrow, and Norton, 101–12.

Chickering, Arthur, and Zelda F. Gamson. 1987. "Seven Principles for Good Practice in Undergraduate Education." *The Wingspread Journal.* Racine, WI: Johnson Foundation. [Available from: The Johnson Foundation, P.O. Box 547, Racine, WI 53401-0547.]

Cole, Ardra L., and J. Gary Knowles. 1993. "Teacher Development Partnership Research: A Focus on Methods and Issues." *American Educational Research Journal* 30: 473–95.

Constable, Hilary. 1994. "Introduction: Change in Classroom Practice: The Need to Know." In Constable, Farrow, and Norton, 1–10.

Constable, Hilary, Steve Farrow, and Jerry Norton, eds. 1994. *Change in Classroom Practice.* Washington, DC: Falmer.

Eble, Kenneth E., and Wilbert J. McKeachie. 1985. *Improving Undergraduate Education through Faculty Development.* San Francisco: Jossey-Bass.

Eblen, C. 1983. "Writing Across the Curriculum: A Survey of University Faculty Views and Classroom Practices." *Research in the Teaching of English* 17.4 (December): 343–48.

Editorial. 1993. *Cincinnati Enquirer* (June 2): A6, column 1.

Finkelstein, Martin J. 1993. "Faculty Vitality in Higher Education." Working paper prepared for the National Center for Education Statistics forum on "Integrating Research on Faculty." Washington, DC. January 10–11. [Used by permission of the author.]

Fishman, Stephen M. 1985. "Writing-to-Learn in Philosophy." *Teaching Philosophy* 8: 331–34.

———. 1989. "Writing and Philosophy." *Teaching Philosophy* 12: 361–74.

———. 1993. "Explicating Our Tacit Tradition: John Dewey and Composition Studies." *College Composition and Communication* 44.3 (October): 315–30.

Fishman, Stephen M., and Lucille P. McCarthy. 1992. "Is Expressivism Dead? Reconsidering Its Romantic Roots and Its Relation to Social Construction." *College English* 54.6 (October): 647–61.

———. 1995. "Community in the Expressivist Classroom: Juggling Liberal and Communitarian Visions." *College English* 57.1 (January): 62–81.

Fulwiler, Toby. 1981. "Showing, Not Telling, at a Writing Workshop." *College English* 43.1 (January): 55–63.

Fulwiler, Toby, and Art Young, eds. 1990. *Programs That Work: Models and Methods for Writing Across the Curriculum.* Portsmouth, NH: Boynton/Cook.

Gitlin, Andrew D. 1990. "Educative Research, Voice, and School Change." *Harvard Educational Review* 60: 443–66.

Goetz, Donna. 1990. "Evaluation of Writing-Across-the-Curriculum Programs." Paper presented at the annual meeting of the American Psychological Association. Boston. August 10–14. ERIC ED 328 917.

Graham, Joan. 1992. "Writing Components, Writing Adjuncts, Writing Links." In McLeod and Soven, 110–33.

Griffin, C. Williams, ed. 1982. Teaching Writing in All Disciplines. New Directions for Teaching and Learning, No. 12. San Francisco: Jossey-Bass.

———. 1985. "Programs for Writing Across the Curriculum: A Report." *College Composition and Communication* 36.4 (December): 398–403.

Hargreaves, Andy. 1988. "Teaching Quality: A Sociological Analysis." *Curriculum Studies* 20: 211–31.

Hargreaves, Andy, and Michael G. Fullan, eds. 1992. *Understanding Teacher Development.* New York: Teachers College Press.

Haring-Smith, Tori. 1992. "Changing Students' Attitudes: Writing Fellows Programs." In McLeod and Soven, 175–88.

Herrington, Anne. 1981. "Writing to Learn: Writing Across the Disciplines." *College English* 43.4 (December): 379–87.

Herrington, Anne, and Charles Moran, eds. 1992. *Writing, Teaching, and Learning in the Disciplines.* New York: Modern Language Association of America.

Hughes-Weiner, Gail, and Susan K. Jensen-Chekalla. 1991. "Organizing a WAC Evaluation Project: Implications for Program Planning." In Stanley and Ambron, 65–70.

Hunt, Linda Lawrence. 1992. *Writing Across the Curriculum.* Spokane, WA: Whitworth College. [In-house publication.]

Hutchings, Pat. 1993. "Lessons from AAHE's Teaching Initiative." In Weimer, 63–66.

Johnstone, Anne C. 1994. *Uses for Journal Keeping: An Ethnography of Writing in a University Science Class.* Revised and edited by Barbara Johnstone and Valerie Balester. Norwood, NJ: Ablex.

Kalmbach, James R., and Michael E. Gorman. 1986. "Surveying Classroom Practices: How Teachers Teach Writing." In *Writing Across the Disciplines: Research into Practice,* edited by Art Young and Toby Fulwiler, 68–85. Upper Montclair, NJ: Boynton/Cook.

Kincheloe, Joe L., and Peter L. McLaren. 1994. "Rethinking Critical Theory and Qualitative Research." In *Handbook of Qualitative Research,* edited by Norman K. Denzin and Yvonna S. Lincoln, 138–57. Thousand Oaks, CA: Sage.

Kipling, Kim J., and Richard J. Murphy Jr. 1992. *Symbiosis: Writing in an Academic Culture.* Portsmouth, NH: Boynton/Cook.

LeCompte, Margaret D., and Judith Preissle Goetz. 1982. "Problems of Reliability and Validity in Ethnographic Research." *Review of Educational Research* 52: 31–60.

Lincoln, Yvonna S., and Egon G. Guba. 1985. *Naturalistic Inquiry.* Beverly Hills, CA: Sage.

Maher, Francis A., and Mary Kay Thomson Tetreault. 1994. *The Feminist Classroom.* New York: Basic Books.

Making Large Classes Interactive. 1995. Videotape. Executive Producers Barbara Walvoord and Leslie Williams. Producer and director H. Michael Sanders. Available from H. Michael Sanders, Director, Media Center, Raymond Walters College of The University of Cincinnati, 9555 Plainfield Rd., Blue Ash, OH 45236. E-mail: h.michael.sanders@uc.edu.

Marsella, Joy, Thomas L. Hilgers, and Clemence McLaren. 1992. "How Students Handle Writing Assignments: A Study of Eighteen Responses in Six Disciplines." In Herrington and Moran, 174–88.

Marshall, James D. "Process and Product: Case Studies of Writing in Two Content Areas." 1984. In *Contexts for Learning to Write: Studies of Secondary School Instruction,* edited by Arthur N. Applebee, 149–68. Norwood, NJ: Ablex.

McCarthy, Lucille. 1991. "Multiple Realities and Multiple Voices in Ethnographic Texts." Paper presented at the annual meeting of the Conference on College Composition and Communication. Boston. March 21–23. ERIC ED 332210.

McCarthy, Lucille P., and Stephen M. Fishman. 1991. "Boundary Conversations: Conflicting Ways of Knowing in Philosophy and Interdisciplinary Research." *Research in the Teaching of English* 25.4 (December): 419–68.

———. 1996. "A Text for Many Voices: Representing Diversity in Reports of Naturalistic Research." In *Ethics and Representation in Qualitative Studies of Literacy,* edited by G. E. Kirsch and Peter Mortensen. Urbana, IL: National Council of Teachers of English.

McCarthy, Lucille P., and Barbara E. Walvoord. 1988. "Models for Collaborative Research in Writing Across the Curriculum." In McLeod, 77–89.

McLeod, Susan H., ed. 1988. *Strengthening Programs for Writing Across the Curriculum.* New Directions for Teaching and Learning, No. 36. San Francisco: Jossey-Bass.

———. 1989. "Writing Across the Curriculum: The Second Stage, and Beyond." *College Composition and Communication* 40.3 (October): 337–43.

McLeod, Susan H., and Susan Shirley. 1988. "National Survey of Writing Across the Curriculum Programs." In McLeod, 103–30.

McLeod, Susan H., and Margot Soven, eds. 1992. *Writing Across the Curriculum: A Guide to Developing Programs.* Newbury Park, CA: Sage.

McMahon, Joan D., ed. 1991. *Teaching Strategies for Writing-Across-the-Curriculum Faculty.* Towson, MD: Towson State University. [In-house publication.]

National Center for Education Statistics. 1995. *National Assessment of College Student Learning: Identifying College Graduates' Essential Skills in Writing, Speech and Listening, and Critical Thinking.* Washington, DC: U.S. Department of Education.

Nelson, Jennie. 1990. "This Was an Easy Assignment: Examining How Students Interpret Academic Writing Tasks." *Research in the Teaching of English* 24.4 (December): 362–96.

North, Stephen M. 1987. *The Making of Knowledge in Composition: Portrait of an Emerging Field.* Upper Montclair, NJ: Boynton/Cook.

Norton, Jerry. 1994. "Primary Teachers Experiencing Change." In Constable, Farrow, and Norton, 127–36.

Nyquist, Jody D. 1993. "The Development of Faculty as Teachers." In Weimer, 989–94.

Palmer, Parker J. 1983. *To Know as We Are Known: A Spirituality of Education.* San Francisco: Harper & Row.

Parker, Robert P., and Vera Goodkin. 1987. *The Consequences of Writing: Enhancing Learning in the Disciplines.* Upper Montclair, NJ: Boynton/Cook.

Raymond, Danielle, Richard Butt, and David Townsend. 1992. "Contexts for Teacher Development: Insights from Teachers' Stories." In Hargreaves and Fullan, 143–61.

Rogers, Everett M. 1983. *The Diffusion of Innovations.* 3rd ed. New York: Free Press.

Russell, David R. 1991. *Writing in the Academic Disciplines, 1870–1990: A Curricular History.* Carbondale: Southern Illinois University Press.

Sipple, JoAnn M. 1987. "Teacher Protocols: A New Evaluation Tool for WAC Programs." Paper presented at the annual meeting of the Conference on College Composition and Communication. Atlanta. March 19–21. ERIC ED 285 150.

Smithson, Isaiah, and Paul Sorrentino. 1987. "Writing Across the Curriculum: An Assessment." *Journal of Teaching Writing* 6: 325–42.

Spradley, James P. 1979. *The Ethnographic Interview.* New York: Holt, Rinehart & Winston.

———. 1980. *Participant Observation.* New York: Holt, Rinehart & Winston.

Stanley, Linda C., and Joanna Ambron, eds. 1991. *Writing Across the Curriculum in Community Colleges.* New Directions for Community Colleges, No. 73. San Francisco: Jossey-Bass.

Steele, Mildred. 1985. "The Development of the Communication Skills Program at Central College, Pella, Iowa." Unpublished document produced at Central College for the Conference on Learning through Communication Skills. November 8. [Available from Barbara Walvoord, Kaneb Center, DeBartolo Hall, Univ. of Notre Dame, Notre Dame, IN 46556.]

Stout, Barbara R., and Joyce N. Magnotto. 1991. "Building on Realities: WAC Programs at Community Colleges." In Stanley and Ambron, 9–13.

Swanson-Owens, Deborah. 1986. "Identifying Natural Sources of Resistance: A Case Study of Implementing Writing Across the Curriculum." *Research in the Teaching of English* 20.1 (February): 69–97.

Swilky, Jody. 1992. "Reconsidering Faculty Resistance to Writing Reform." *WPA: Writing Program Administration* 16.1/2 (Fall/Winter): 50–60.

Thaiss, Christopher, ed. 1983. *Writing to Learn: Essays and Reflections on Writing Across the Curriculum.* Dubuque, IA: Kendall-Hunt.

Walvoord, Barbara E. 1997. (in press). "From Conduit to Customer: The Role of WAC Faculty in WAC Assessment." In *Assessing Writing Across the Curriculum: Diverse Approaches and Practices,* edited by Kathleen Yancey and Brian Huot. Norwood, NJ: Ablex.

———. 1996. "The Future of Writing Across the Curriculum." *College English* 58.1 (January): 58–79.

Walvoord, Barbara E., and John Bryan. 1995. "How Students Learn Decision-Making in a Computer Networked Course: An Ethnographic Study." Paper presented at the annual meeting of the Conference on College Composition and Communication. Washington, DC. March 24.

Walvoord, Barbara E., and H. Fil Dowling Jr., with John Breihan, Virginia Johnson Gazzam, Carl E. Henderson, Gertrude B. Hopkins, Barbara Mallonee, and Sally McNelis. 1990. "The Baltimore Area Consortium." In Fulwiler and Young, 273–86.

Walvoord, Barbara E., and Lucille P. McCarthy, with Virginia Johnson Anderson, John R. Breihan, Susan Miller Robison, and A. Kimbrough Sherman. 1991. *Thinking and Writing in College: A Naturalistic Study of Students in Four Disciplines.* Urbana, IL: National Council of Teachers of English.

Weimer, Maryellen, ed. 1993. *Faculty as Teachers: Taking Stock of What We Know.* University Park: National Center on Postsecondary Teaching, Learning, and Assessment, Pennsylvania State University.

Index

Authors

Barbara E. Walvoord is director of the Kaneb Center for Teaching and Learning and (concurrent) professor of English at the University of Notre Dame. She was formerly director of Writing Across the Curriculum, co-director of the Project to Improve and Reward Teaching, and professor of English at the University of Cincinnati. She was the 1987 Maryland Teacher of the Year in English higher education. She has founded and directed three writing-across-the-curriculum programs and a regional consortium, each of which has won national recognition. She leads faculty workshops on teaching, writing, and assessment nationwide. Her publications include *Thinking and Writing in College: A Naturalistic Study of Students in Four Disciplines* (NCTE, 1991).

Linda Lawrence Hunt is associate professor in the English department at Whitworth College, where she directs its WAC and composition programs and team teaches in the CORE program. She is a doctoral candidate at Gonzaga University. During 1989–1991, she administered the CAPHE/Murdock grant, which brought Barbara Walvoord on campus to lead writing workshops for faculty. During those two years, almost two-thirds of Whitworth's faculty participated in one- to five-day workshop opportunities. Many of these faculty taught in the newly instituted W-I-designated courses. A freelance writer, she has authored or co-authored four books and numerous articles that have appeared in regional and national publications.

H. Fil Dowling Jr. is professor of English at Towson State University. Since the early 1980s, he has coordinated Towson State's WAC program. In 1985, he founded the Faculty Writers' Response Group for Towson State faculty. A founding member of the Baltimore Area Consortium for Writing Across the Curriculum, he was its coordinator from 1987 to 1990. He was on the Executive Board of the Maryland Council of Teachers of English from 1984 to 1990 and served as editor of the *Maryland English Journal*, an NCTE affiliate journal, from 1985 to 1990. The author of several journal articles (including two in *College Composition and Communication*) and a book chapter co-written with Barbara Walvoord on composition-related subjects, he also has given many conference papers on composition, on using journals and writing-to-learn in literature classes, and on American realist authors and women authors.

Joan D. McMahon holds an M.A. in health education and a doctorate in education from George Washington University. She has taught health science at Towson State University since 1973. At Towson, she has supervised the health science student teaching program and the Wellness in the Workplace Program. Currently, she is the project director of the University Teaching Initiative. She also advises and teaches in the Human Resource Development graduate program. She is the author of several student manuals on teaching, a monograph on writing-across-the-curriculum strategies, a monograph on faculty roles and rewards, and numerous publications appearing in health education journals about the teaching/learning process.

Contributors

Virginia Slachman worked as Barbara Walvoord's research assistant during the academic year 1993–1994, conducting and analyzing interviews with University of Cincinnati professors from diverse disciplines. In March 1994, these findings were presented by Tami Phenix, Lisa Udel, Barbara Walvoord, and Slachman at the Conference on College Composition and Communication. She is the author of *The Lance and Rita Poems,* a collection recently recorded by Aspen Stage. She received her Ph.D. from the University of Cincinnati in 1996.

Lisa Udel received her B.A. in English from the University of Michigan in 1985 and her M.A. in English from Indiana University in 1989. She is currently a doctoral candidate at the University of Cincinnati, working on her dissertation, which examines representations of Native Americans in the literature of twentieth-century women writers and also examines Native American feminism. She served as the research assistant to Barbara Walvoord, the University of Cincinnati's WAC director, during the academic year 1992–1993. She has also published in *MELUS.*